WHEN HEAVY BECAME MASS

WHEN HEAVY BECAME MASS

HEAVY MUSIC 1970-2000

FREDD CARROLL

Left Eye Lazy Publishing

Published by Left Eye Lazy Publishing

ISBN 978-1-972440-00-1 (Hardcover)
ISBN 978-1-972440-01-8 (Paperback)
ISBN 978-1-972440-02-5 (eBook)

For Alyssa, Anthony, and Riley

Foreword vii

CHAPTER ONE 12

OPTIMISM 1

ECONOMICS 8

TECHNOLOGICAL ACCELERATION 12

AUDIENCE RECEPTION 17

MUTATION CONSEQUENCE 22

CHAPTER TWO 29

THE SECOND WAVE (1977-1980) 30

THE INFRASTRUCTURE IS BUILT (1979-1982) 34

CHAPTER THREE 50

ARENA EXPANSION (1970–1976) 51

LABEL INVESTMENT (1970–1976) 58

TOURING CIRCUITS (1971–1976) 64

GEOGRAPHIC HOMOGENIZATION (1971–1976).. 71

MEDIA STANDARDIZATION (1972–1976) 77

CHAPTER FOUR 85

ACCESS OVER SKILL (1974–1977) 86

SCENE OVER CIRCUIT (1975–1978) 93

IDEOLOGY OVER ATMOSPHERE (1976–1978) 99

PUNK'S INTERNAL INSTABILITY (1977–1979) 108

CHAPTER FIVE 120

SPEED AS ESCALATION (1978–1982) 121

MILITANCY OVER AMBIGUITY (1979–1982) 127

REINFORCEMENT THROUGH WEIGHT (1982–1985)
.... 133

THRASH AS SYNTHESIS (1983–1986) 141

CHAPTER SIX 148

MUTATION WITHOUT A CENTER (1984–1989)... 149

EXTREMITY ARMS RACE (1987–1990) 157

UNDERGROUND INFRASTRUCTURE EXPLOSION

.... 166

NO CENTER HOLDS (1988–1992) 174

CHAPTER SEVEN 186

THE NEW CENTER (1983–1991) 187

ENGINEERING THE SOUND (1983-1991) 192

WAS IT REAL METAL? (1983-1991)......................... 199

THE THRONE BREAKS (1988-1992) 209

CHAPTER EIGHT 221

THE LAST THRONE (1991-1992) 222

THE AUSTERITY WEAPON (1991-1992) 227

THE CEILING BUILT (1992-1996) 232

CHAPTER NINE 240

HOSTILE AUTHORITY (1992-1996)......................... 241

THE FORTRESS & THE LABORATORY (1991-1998)

.... 245

THE LAST RECOMBINATION (1996-2000) 253

MULTIPOLAR PERMANENCE (1998-2000) 260

Foreword

I was born in 1969, which means I came to consciousness at precisely the moment when the story this book tells was beginning to unfold. I didn't know that at the time. Nobody does when they're living inside history. You just know that something is happening and that it matters and that you want to be as close to it as possible.

Music found me early and found me completely. My four parents — biological and steps — each played a role in that finding, but my stepmother's record collection was where it started. The Turtles. The Beatles. Bowie. Vinyl stacked and catalogued with the casual authority of someone who understood that records were not background noise but primary objects. The things that deserved attention and rewarded the attention you gave them. And I gave them hours. Not listening in the passive sense that the word implies but reading — the inner sleeves, the liner notes, the production credits, the photographs, the specific visual language that each record used to communicate who it was and what it was for before the needle hit the groove. I was learning something without knowing I was learning it. Music was an artifact with history and context. With a set of decisions behind it, and that understanding the decisions was part of understanding the music.

Then Kiss hit me. Late 1970s. I was nine or ten years old and completely unprepared for what was about to happen.

Kiss didn't just enter my listening life — they bit me, devoured me, and changed the relationship between me and sound forever. The volume. The image. The specific theatrical authority of a band that understood instinctively that heaviness was not just a sonic property but a physical, visual, and psychological event. An event that happened to the audience rather than being received by them. I didn't have the analytical vocabulary for any of this at nine years old. I had the experience, which is what the vocabulary is built to describe and what no vocabulary can fully replace.

By fourteen I was in a recording studio with my thrash band Born Dead. We didn't make it. Most bands don't. But the experience of being inside the recording process of understanding from the inside how the decisions are made, and how the sound that ends up on the record, is the product of choices. Between the arrangement, tone, production, and performance, how the room and the console and the engineer are all part of the instrument. This gave me something that years of listening alone couldn't have provided. It gave me the practitioner's understanding, the knowledge of what the music costs to make and what it requires and what it feels like when the decisions are right and when they aren't.

After Born Dead I remained musical and remained multi-genre. I like what I like. Metal has always been 1A and the form I often return to. The form whose history I find most analytically interesting and whose development across the thirty years this book covers tells the most complete. A structurally coherent story about what music does to people and what people do to music. But the Beatles and Bowie never left. The inner sleeves and liner notes never stopped mattering. The understanding that music exists inside a context of economic, infrastructural, cultural, psychological and that the context shapes the music as surely as the musicians do. This has been with me since my stepmother's record collection, whether I could articulate it or not.

I have written fiction across multiple genres and published it. In 2024 I began Headbangers History, a YouTube channel that reignited the historical side of my relationship with heavy music and made explicit what had been implicit for years. That the story of how heavy music developed was a story I wanted to tell and that the tools I had developed as a writer of fiction were the right tools for telling it. The story requires narrative intelligence as much as historical knowledge.

The three years that produced this book were not years of academic research in the conventional sense. They were years of reading rockstar biographies, touring budgets books, band management guides, contract analyses, infrastructure histories, and the specific practical literature of how the music industry operates. Every level from the club circuit to the arena to the major label to the DIY pressing plant. I was not trying to build a chronological history of heavy metal. That book has multiple versions and some of those versions are excellent. I was trying to understand the forces among the economic forces. The infrastructural forces, the social and psychological forces that turned heaviness from a local mutation in Birmingham in 1970 into a global condition. By the century's close it had embedded itself in more distinct communities across more geographic and cultural contexts than any other form of popular music.

The existing literature on heavy metal is substantial and in places genuinely brilliant. The biographies capture the human texture of specific moments with an intimacy that no analytical framework can replicate. The chronological histories establish the factual record with necessary precision. The cultural studies scholarship examines the sociological and political dimensions of the form's development with theoretical style. What I found missing across most of it was the structural argument. The attempt to explain not just what happened but why it had to happen. Why do the specific mutations occur in the specific sequence they did? Why the escalation logic ran the way it ran, why the controls always generated the fragmentations that followed them. Why the commercial mainstream and the underground kept producing each other in an endless cycle of opposition and absorption that neither system ever fully understood while it was living through it.

That structural argument is what this book attempts. The bands are evidence. The records are documents. The scenes are case studies in how specific human communities respond to specific economic and cultural pressures through the medium of organized sound. The people are the subject

— the musicians and the audiences and the label executives and the engineers and the promoters and the zine writers and the tape traders, all of them operating within infrastructures they didn't design. While responding to pressures they didn't choose and produced through the specific combination of talent, necessity, and historical accident. Creative work always involves something that outlasted every individual contribution and became larger than the sum of its parts.

I was nine years old when Kiss bit me. I am in my fifties now and the bite has not healed, and I have no interest in healing it. This book is what the bite produced. Thirty years of living inside heavy music and three years of trying to understand what I had been living inside. All assembled into an argument about why the music that hit me at nine years old was not a phase or a preference or a cultural accident. It was a permanent force that was always going to find me because it was always going to find everyone who needed it.

Everyone who needs it knows who they are.

This book is for them.

CHAPTER ONE

When Optimism Broke

OPTIMISM

Optimism didn't fade. It failed under pressure.

Late 1960s rock was built on expansion, and for a moment that expansion felt sincere. Psychedelia promised something close to a divine existence. The counterculture aimed at liberation and believed music could deliver it. The Grateful Dead stretched songs into open-ended jams with no interest in ending. The Beatles abandoned pop craft entirely and retreated into the studio, emerging with Sgt. Pepper as proof that rock could be an art. The prevailing belief was simple: consciousness could be widened through volume, LSD, and a chord that resolved upward. The major key was a worldview.

That optimism had conditions. It required postwar confidence and the belief that growth was permanent. By 1969, both were cracking. Vietnam had expanded far beyond its original justification. Televised combat pulled the war out of the newspaper and into the living room — no delay, no editorial distance, just the footage. The 1968 assassinations of Martin Luther King Jr. and Robert Kennedy didn't just remove two men. They removed the credibility of reform itself. Then Altamont arrived in December 1969 — a spectator killed during a Rolling Stones set while Hells Angels swung pool cues at the crowd. The idea that the counterculture represented peace didn't survive the night. Expansion no longer felt like a direction. It felt like a lie that had finally been caught.

In Britain, the tension had a different texture, and a harder one. Birmingham was industrial, still carrying the disfigurement of wartime bombing, economically uneven in ways that London's media never bothered to report. Factory labor didn't just define daily life. It consumed it. The paycheck wasn't an ambition, it was survival. There was no San Francisco equivalent here. No Haight-Ashbury, no art school optimism, no chemical mysticism. Black Sabbath didn't emerge from that world. They emerged from metal presses, unemployment lines, and the desperation that comes from watching your options narrow before you're old enough to have exercised them. The world outside their rehearsal space wasn't backdrop. It was material.

The collision point was plain: psychedelic optimism just couldn't manage industrial dread. They were two completely different terrains whose goodwill didn't connect them. Music and technology had never touched ground at the same time — heavier gear, darker culture, and a lyrical language still singing about peace while the world it depicted had already fallen apart. The PA stacks grew larger. The distortion thickened. But the lexicon of liberation wasn't sufficient to hold the weight of what people were being held up against. The words and the sound were no longer the same conversation. By the late 1960s Marshall stacks were basic tools, not frills. Volume wasn't a statement anymore. It was an expectation. And along with that normalization came an arms race that had less to do with vision than with physics. Bands pushed output, because the rooms wanted it, and the rooms wanted it because people had grown accustomed to feeling sound as much as hearing it. Without a purpose, louder sounds become pressure. Without a clear sense of direction, pressure takes on the threatening aspect. Something had to give. If the culture were darker, and the gear heavier, the music caught between them couldn't preserve its original shape. It had to absorb both forces and make movement. The only question was what that direction looked like—and what band would define it first. Black Sabbath's self-titled debut in February 1970 answered the question nobody had formally asked. The opening track builds on a tritone — an interval instinctively avoided in rock harmony because it refuses resolution. It doesn't land anywhere comfortably. It hangs there, destabilizing everything beneath it. Tony Iommi didn't choose that interval from theory. He arrived at it through necessity. A factory accident had cost him the tips of two fingers on his fretting hand. To keep playing, he detuned his guitar to reduce string tension and fitted his damaged fingers with homemade prosthetics. The detuning wasn't aesthetic rebellion. It was a practical workaround that happened to lower the pitch, loosen the strings, and thicken the attack into something that had never quite existed before.

Geezer Butler's bass didn't walk around the riff melodically — it doubled it, locked in, immovable. Bill Ward played fills that felt like interruptions rather than support, destabilizing the groove rather than anchoring it. Ozzy Osbourne didn't project ecstasy or liberation. He sounded cornered. None of these were conscious stylistic choices assembled in a rehearsal room discussion. They were adaptive responses to conditions. The physical, economic, and geographic conditions that no other band shared in quite the same combination.

The results compounded each other. Detuning born from injury produced a tone with industrial gravity. A lower, thicker, heavier than anything that the blues framework had generated before. Slowing the tempo removed the dance function entirely. With it went the implicit promise that the music was there to make you feel better. The tritone, held at volume through a Marshall stack, didn't resolve. It accumulated. And what accumulated was dread. Not performed dread, but something structural. Inevitable. The kind that doesn't announce itself because it doesn't need to.

The mutation solved a problem nobody had articulated: how do you make amplified rock music reflect social collapse rather than simply protest it? Dissent still believes in the possibility of change. Collapse doesn't. Sabbath weren't rallying anyone. They were documenting a weight their audience already knew by feel.

Geography makes the argument concrete. Birmingham's working-class infrastructure didn't just provide context; it provided a template. The band rehearsed near factories. Iommi has spoken repeatedly about the sound of metal presses as a formative presence, something that worked its way into his instincts before he could name it. This isn't mythology built after this fact. It is the result of an environment shaping the people inside it. The industrial city produced industrial rhythm. A repetitive, heavy, indifferent to resolution. Iommi absorbed it in the way anyone absorbs the dominant sound of the place they grew up. It simply became the only rhythm that felt honest.

The mutation didn't stop at sound. It rewrote the subject matter entirely. "War Pigs" didn't gesture vaguely at conflict. It targeted political leadership directly. "Electric Funeral" took nuclear extinction and treated it not as distant nightmare but as a logical outcome. The psychedelic era had dealt in abstraction with fear as a feeling to be dissolved, anxiety as something music could lift you above. Sabbath removed that option. They named the specific things that were coming. The apocalyptic wasn't a mood anymore. It was a location. Fear stopped being something you floated through and became something you stood inside.

Heavy music was not inevitable. That argument deserves honest examination before it gets dismissed. Led Zeppelin and Deep Purple were already pushing amplified blues into a harder territory. A reasonable case exists that Sabbath was simply a louder entry in a crowded British hard rock field with a darker mood but not firmly different.

I don't accept that. Here's why.

Zeppelin built their heaviness on sexuality and groove. The riff as seduction, the rhythm as something your body follows without being asked. Deep Purple anchored theirs in virtuosity, classical architecture bleeding into rock muscle. Both bands, for all their volume and force, still resolved upward. They still offered release. The tension they built existed in service of a payoff. That payoff — that upward resolution — was the entire blues inheritance from which they were working.

Sabbath removed it. They didn't accelerate the tempo, they buried it. They didn't highlight solos, they orbited riffs. They didn't build toward release. They built toward further weight. That isn't a difference of degree. That is a difference of architecture. Zeppelin rewards you for staying with it. Deep Purple dazzles you. Sabbath refuses to do either. It holds the dread in place and asks you to sit with it. No other band in that field was making that demand.

Consider the alternative. If the counterculture had stabilized. Let's say no Altamont, Vietnam cleanly resolved, postwar economic confidence holding. Then hard rock continues toward technical ambition rather than the tonal weight. Progressive rock was already waiting in that lane. Yes, and Emerson, Lake & Palmer carried complexity instead of heaviness. With intricate time signatures, keyboard orchestration, fantasy themes that offered escape rather than confrontation. In a more stable cultural climate, that version of amplified music may have dominated the decade. Heavy metal, if it emerged at all, might have remained a blues-rock variation. A louder version without the structural mutation that made it something genuinely new.

But the early 1970's didn't cooperate with optimism. Britain's economic decline deepened through 1973. Industrial strikes widened. Youth unemployment climbed in exactly the cities where Sabbath's audience lived. The records sold and kept selling. Not because they were a novelty, but because the audience recognized something the cultural mainstream wasn't offering them. The mutation didn't just happen. It was validated, continuously, by people who needed it to exist.

The people who responded weren't buying a cultural statement. They were buying something that sounded like the life they were already living. It's not a reflection of it, but rather the actual weight of it pressed into vinyl. The working-class audience didn't need the music explained to them. They recognize it the way you recognize your own street.

Sabbath created the template: down-tuned riff, minor tonality, apocalyptic subject matter. That structure didn't just define a sound; it built a skeleton. Every subsequent mutation could attach itself to it. Speed could increase without losing weight because the foundation was already established. Aggression could escalate because the architecture could hold it. Without Sabbath's collapse of optimism into riff-based dread, the extremity that followed has nothing load bearing to grow from.

The system didn't choose darkness because it wanted a new direction. It chose darkness because the previous configuration had run out of things to stand on. The ground beneath psychedelic optimism had been eroding since 1968. Altamont just made it visible.

The culture didn't want darkness. It simply ran out of ways to avoid it.

But sound alone doesn't explain the full mutation. Beneath the cultural collapse and geographic isolation, there was a harder and more specific pressure driving everything. The kind that doesn't show up in music theory or counterculture timelines. It shows up on a pay slip.

ECONOMICS

The collapse of optimism wasn't theoretical. It had a pay slip attached to it.

Postwar Britain had sold a specific promise of steadiness, reconstruction, and a future that rewarded their patience. By the late 1960's that promise was visibly weakening. Heavy industry was declining not gradually but structurally. Automation cut labor in manufacturing cities faster than any alternative could absorb it. Birmingham was built on steel, automotive production, and factory output. The people were now watching those foundations destabilize in real time. Strikes were increasing. The Industrial Relations Act debates exposed how raw the friction between labor and government had become. The working-class security net wasn't fraying at the edges. It was tearing at the center.

A generation raised on the expectation of rebuilding was now staring at the reduction. Not abstract anxiety, but the concrete weight of a paycheck that may not arrive next month.

The tension intensified because the cultural messaging refused to acknowledge it. London's media was still selling Swinging London filled with boutiques, optimism, the idea that Britain was modern and ascending. Psychedelic ideology was still packaging freedom as something available to anyone willing to tune in. But in the Midlands, none of that translated into anything tangible. There were no boutiques. There were metal presses and machinery and the silence of a factory floor running fewer shifts than it did last year. When the cultural story being told and the economic reality being lived departs that sharply, the friction looks for somewhere to go. When it finds music that carries the weight of that separation rather than denying it, the correction is immediate and instinctive.

Black Sabbath were not art-school experimentalists. They were factory laborers and that distinction matters beyond biography. Iommi's industrial accident and the detuning it produced has already been established. What hasn't been examined is what that injury represents inside a broader economic situation. It wasn't an isolated event. It was the kind of thing that happened to people in Birmingham in 1965. Workplace injury was a routine consequence of factory labor, and factory labor was what you did when the other options had already closed. The sound that came out of that accident wasn't just one man's adaptation. It was the sound of an entire class of people whose bodies were shaped by the work they had no choice of performing.

These were young men who had been handed a specific script. That script said work hard, the factory provides, stability follows. By 1969 the factory was lying to them. That betrayal didn't produce protest songs. It produced something quieter and heavier than protest. It produced people who had stopped expecting the arc to bend.

The economic backdrop also explains the tempo. Factory work is repetitive and slow-moving — not in a pondering sense, but in the sense of hours that grind without release. Sabbath's riffs don't swing like Chicago blues because the environment they came from never suggested dancing as an option. Listen to "Behind the Wall of Sleep." The groove isn't built for movement. It's built for endurance. Butler's bass and Ward's fills make more sense when you understand that instability wasn't a stylistic choice. This was a faithful reproduction of what economic instability feels like from the inside. Not chaos. Just the constant low-level sensation that the ground beneath you isn't entirely solid.

The mutation was predictable because the musical framework it replaced had an assumption built in that no longer held. Blues-rock believed in mobility, that tension exists, but it also resolves. The chord returns home. The release is coming. That belief requires faith that things can improve, that the arc bends somewhere better. In a city where economic upward motion had stalled, and that harmonic promises didn't just sound hollow. They sounded dishonest. Sabbath removed the resolution because the resolution would have been a lie. The riff doesn't go anywhere because the life it reflected wasn't going anywhere either. When the music finally matched that reality, the audience didn't need to be convinced. They simply recognized it.

The counterargument deserves acknowledgment. Economic decline doesn't automatically produce heavy music. If it did, every struggling industrial region would have generated its own version of metal, and that clearly didn't happen. Hardship is common. Sabbath is not. Economic pressure alone isn't a sufficient explanation.

What made Birmingham specifically generative was the convergence of three factors. First, a concentrated industrial soundscape that provided an unconscious rhythmic education. A mechanical repetition with no swing, no release, no resolution. Second, proximity to London's recording infrastructure. Regent Sound and the capital's studio network gave Midlands bands access to equipment and production capability unavailable in a regional isolation. Without that access, Sabbath's sound may never have been captured with enough force to travel. Third, amplifier technology had matured. Marshall stacks were available, normalized, and capable of delivering the low-end weight that down-tuned heaviness required to land as a physical force rather than thin noise.

Hardship alone doesn't transform. Hardship plus the right structural conditions does.

Consider the alternative. If Birmingham's economy had remained stable with its employment steady, industry intact, the postwar promise was holding true. Then Sabbath may have drifted toward blues virtuosity the way Zeppelin did. Iommi's injury might still have produced detuning, but without economic dread saturating every lyrical instinct, the subject matter may have stayed heavy in tone without becoming apocalyptic in content. The riffs might have carried weight without carrying meaning. Metal might have emerged as technical hard rock. Being impressive, loud, but without the doom-laden gravity that made it something categorically new.

Instead, the injury landed inside industrial decay and cultural abandonment at the same time. That coming together produced something that couldn't have been designed. And its consequence extended well beyond 1970. The template Sabbath established was that heaviness could encode economic despair directly into its structure. Proving replicable every time the same conditions reappeared. The late 1970s recession and the NWOBHM. The 1980s Rust Belt collapse and American thrash. The pattern repeated because the conditions repeated.

Heavy music didn't appear because musicians decided darkness was more interesting. It appeared because the economic floor dropped, and the sound had no choice but to carry what the floor left behind.

But economic pressure only explains what the music needed to say. It doesn't fully explain how it said it with that force. For that, you must look at what was happening to the gear because technology wasn't just keeping pace with the darkness. It was accelerating ahead of it.

TECHNOLOGICAL ACCELERATION

By the late 1960s, amplification had outpaced the belief it was supposed to serve.

Marshall stacks were no longer a novelty they were standard touring equipment. PA systems had scaled to manage festival crowds at Hyde Park and the Isle of Wight. Distortion had moved from accident to expectation, from a byproduct of pushing equipment too hard to a texture audiences now anticipated and demanded. Technology had matured faster than the cultural framework around it. Volume capabilities had exceeded the lyrical language designed to justify them. The gear was saying something the songs hadn't caught up to yet.

Psychedelia had used volume as a perceptual tool. Cream and the Jimi Hendrix Experience pushed distortion into vivid, vast territory. But it kept tethering to blues-based liberation. The loudness served the ecstasy. It was in the employment of a worldview that believed bigger sound meant higher consciousness, that volume itself was a vehicle for excellence.

By 1969, the rigs were heavier than their worldview could support.

Altamont made it undeniable. A massive PA system, a massive crowd, no structural control. Technology didn't elevate the event; it amplified its chaos. The promise that scale equaled greatness broke down publicly and violently. What the gear delivered that night wasn't consciousness expansion. It was a demonstration of what happens when volume outgrows the philosophy trying to contain it.

The amplification didn't respond to that collapse by shrinking. It kept accelerating. Louder amps, thicker cabinets, more sustained low-end echo. If cultural positivity could no longer justify that weight, something else had to. The sound needed a view that could hold it.

Black Sabbath adapted first and more deliberately than they're often credited.

Iommi ran his down-tuned guitar through Laney Supergroup amps. With a high headroom, aggressive midrange response that signal chain, combined with the lower pitch his detuning produced, generated a low-frequency density. It didn't shimmer through a full stack. It projected. This wasn't accidental tonal discovery. It was a particular instrument, a particular tuning, and a particular amplifier finding each other at the right moment.

Worth stopping on that detail. Iommi didn't use Marshall stacks. The London-built equipment that had become the British rock standard. He used Laney. Laney was a Birmingham company, founded locally, built locally. The gear Sabbath played through wasn't imported from the capital's rock foundation. It came from the same city, the same economic landscape, the same industrial environment as the band. Birmingham did not just shape the sound. It amplified it.

Physics matter. At high wattage, low frequencies stop being something you hear and become something you feel. A minor-key riff played slowly through a high-wattage amp doesn't just fill a room. It creates pressure. Sabbath structured their riffs to exploit exactly that. The tritone on their debut doesn't resolve, and through high-volume amplification it doesn't need to. It sustains, vibrating at a frequency the body registers before the mind can label it. The space between notes matters as much as the notes themselves because the amplifier fills that space with harmonic decay and controlled noise. Blues-rock filled space with fast runs and solos. Density through speed. Sabbath slowed everything down because the technology had matured enough to let sustain carry the tension instead. Amplifier gain replaced musical density. The gear did the work the notes didn't need to.

Sabbath's debut was recorded at Regent Sound in a single session. Equipment is basic, the process is rapid. The rawness wasn't a limitation they worked around. It was a technological truth. The sound of a band playing at full force with no buffer between what they were and what the tape received. The recording chain didn't dress the music up. It documented the weight.

The mutation was inevitable because amplification past a certain threshold creates a demand the music must answer. Once the gear reaches a size where sound is physically imposing, the music either becomes more complex to justify the scale or heavier to match it. Those are the only two directions. Progressive rock took the first. Sabbath took the second. In the cultural moment of 1970, weight was the more honest answer.

The February 1970 release proved something nobody had demonstrated before. That a slow minimal riff could dominate radio and concert venues if the amplification behind it was massive. Difficulty had always been the assumed requirement for scale. Sabbath removed that assumption. Technology didn't need decoration. It needed weight. Simplicity, at sufficient volume, was a weapon.

The counterargument is worth sitting with. Loud gear existed well before 1970. The Who were destroying Marshall stacks in 1967. Hendrix was maxing amplifiers that same year. If the technology was already there, why didn't metal emerge then?

Because volume alone doesn't transform. What transforms is volume combined with intent. The intent is shaped by social pressure. Hendrix used high gain as a vehicle for psychedelic grace, squeezing color and liberation out of distortion. Townshend used it for kinetic force, the power chord as a punctuation on a generation's restlessness. Both were accelerating while pushing energy upward and outward. The technology in their hands served growth.

Sabbath decelerated. They took the same gear and pointed it in the opposite direction. The distortion Hendrix used to soar became the distortion Sabbath used to sink. The same technology, under different social pressures produces an entirely different structure. The gear didn't change between 1967 and 1970. The world it was being played into did.

Consider the alternative. If amplification had plateaued — smaller venues, lower wattage, limited PA development. Sabbath's slow minimal riffs would have sounded thin and unconvincing. The doom architecture depends entirely on sustained low-end presence. Without the physical weight that high-wattage amplification provides, the space between notes is just silence rather than tension. Slow simplicity requires sustained power. Without it, heavy metal may never have separated from fast blue rock because speed was the only other way to generate energy, and speed was already spoken for.

Instead, amplification kept scaling. Distortion became standardized. Once normalized, conflict loses its shock value and becomes a structural option rather than a offense. Once conflict stabilizes, darkness can be arranged rather than merely stumbled on. The technological ceiling kept rising, and aggression scaled with it. Each generation of gear enabling a degree of limit the previous ceiling couldn't have supported.

When the gear gets heavier, the structure that follows gets heavier too. You cannot run freedom philosophy through industrial-grade wattage indefinitely. Physics eventually demands a design that matches the force being generated. Technological acceleration didn't create heavy music on its own. It simply made it impossible to remain light.

But technology only takes the argument so far. The gear created the conditions. The culture and the economics created the need. What neither explains is why a specific audience chose to meet that sound and claim it as their own. That choice wasn't passive. It was deliberate. And it changed everything that came after.

AUDIENCE RECEPTION

The collapse of optimism wasn't complete until the audience chose to meet it.

The counterculture claimed to speak for an entire generation but by 1969 that generation had fractured along lines the movement never acknowledged. University students and media-connected youth were deepening their investment in psychedelic narratives. The idea that liberation was available to anyone willing to pursue it. In industrial cities like Birmingham, that story had no purchase. Working-class youth weren't experimenting with consciousness expansion. They were navigating mass layoffs, diminishing factory shifts, and the slow realization that the future they'd been promised was not arriving. When the cultural script insists that freedom is expanding while the reality lived delivers the opposite, resentment doesn't announce itself. It accumulates. And it looks for something to attach to.

By 1969 the accumulation was complete. Vietnam, the assassinations, and Altamont each had been processed individually as the news arrived. But by the end of the decade, they had compounded into something harder to dismiss. The idea that the culture was moving forward had stopped feeling like shared belief and started feeling like a management strategy. Something being repeated loudly enough to drown out the evidence. For working-class youth specifically, the gap between the official narrative and daily reality had become too wide to dismiss. The resentment had nowhere left to go until the music gave it somewhere tangible.

When Black Sabbath released their debut in February 1970, the critical response was dismissal. Crude. Primitive. A regression from the sophistication that rock had spent the late 1960's building toward. The gatekeepers heard it and found it wanting.

The audience heard it and bought it immediately.

Contemporary reviews described the debut as humorless and dull. Music for people who had given up on the idea that rock could be divine. That characterization was meant as judgment. It turned out to be an accurate description of exactly why the audience needed it.

The album reached the UK Top 10 without critical support, without media enthusiasm, without the method that was supposed to determine what mattered. Paranoid followed later that year and hit number one. That gap between what the critics said the music was worth and what the public decided it was worth is not a footnote. It is the evidence. When an audience overrules its gatekeepers that firmly and that quickly, something real is being communicated. The music had found the people it was made for before anyone in a position of cultural authority had given them permission to want it.

The reason isn't complicated. Sabbath's sound matched an emotional reality more accurately than anything the psychedelic era had offered. The slow riffs, the minor tonality, the apocalyptic subject matter did not offer escape. It offered acknowledgment. And acknowledgment, when you have been living inside something the surrounding culture refuses to name, is an extraordinarily powerful thing. The music wasn't telling the audience that things would improve. It was telling them that what they were feeling was real. That was enough. In some cases, it was everything.

The audience that claimed Sabbath didn't look like the counterculture. No flowing fabrics, no floral prints, no visual language borrowed from Eastern religion. Instead, denim and leather. Band patches sewn onto jackets worn to actual work. The aesthetic rejection was as deliberate as the musical one. A working-class uniform that said this audience had never belonged to the movement now collapsing.

The physical response confirmed it. Concert reports from 1970 describe crowds that weren't dancing the way blues audiences danced, weren't swaying the way psychedelic audiences swayed. They were standing and absorbing it with heads down, bodies locked into the weight of the sound. That shift in physical behavior reflects a structural change in what the music was asking. Heavy amplification combined with slow riff architecture produces immersion rather than release. The audience doesn't rise above the sound. It endures it. For a working-class youth that had spent years enduring things they had no control over, that demand felt less like a burden than like recognition.

The sales figures weren't a coincidence. When cultural optimism fractured, the audience doesn't disappear. It redirects. If the market is saturated with expansion narratives during a period of genuine reduction, a demand gap opens. It may not be visible to the people running the cultural operation, because they're still looking at what sold last year. But it is there, and something will fill it. Paranoid, reaching number one during a narrowing UK economy was the audience voting with its money for the art that was telling them the truth about where they actually were.

The counterargument: Sabbath succeeded on shock value alone. Occult imagery, horror themes, the novelty of something deliberately ugly in a market chasing beauty. Curiosity sells. Sin attracts attention. The audience wasn't responding to emotional truth. They were drawn to the spectacle.

The durability answers it. Shock fades and the audience moves on to the next irritation. But by 1971 Sabbath were headlining internationally. "Paranoid" and "Iron Man" became radio staples rather than novelties, returning to rotation long after any shock value should have expired. Sustained chart presence and touring power are not the fingerprints of a gimmick. They are the fingerprints of an audience that kept coming back because the music kept delivering something they needed.

The reception patterns confirm it further. Yes, and Emerson, Lake & Palmer were building genuine complexity for art-school audiences during the same period. And that lane thrived. Its own devoted following, its own commercial success, its own cultural momentum. But it didn't absorb Sabbath's audience, and Sabbath's audience didn't migrate toward it. Two separate markets ran parallel without significant overlapping. That separation reflects two genuinely different audiences with two genuinely unique needs. The music that met those needs was structurally different because the needs themselves were differing.

If the counterculture had maintained its hold on working-class youth. And if Vietnam had de-escalated cleanly, the economic pressure had eased before it reached critical mass then Sabbath's bleak minimalism may have found only a cult audience. The critics who dismissed them might have shaped public conversation more effectively. Heavy metal might have been categorized as horror rock, a novelty lane, briefly interesting but secondary.

Instead, the audience overruled its gatekeepers. And once it proved there was genuine mass appetite for heaviness without resolution, the infrastructure responded. Not because anyone in power had decided darkness deserved investment but because the numbers made the argument impossible to ignore. The next generation of heavy bands didn't have to establish from scratch that this music could find an audience. That work had already been done in 1970 by the people buying Paranoid in a collapsing economy without permission.

The system doesn't move because critics approve. It moves because crowds choose what reflects them. When optimism collapsed, the audience didn't retreat into something softer. They turned the volume up and refused to come back down.

But the audience's choice didn't just validate the mutation. It locked it in place. And once something is locked in place with that kind of commercial force behind it, the question stops asking whether it will survive. It becomes what it will produce. What Sabbath built in 1970 wasn't just a sound. It was a foundation. And foundations don't stay empty for long.

MUTATION CONSEQUENCE

When Black Sabbath embedded dread into the architecture of rock music in 1970, they didn't add a darker flavor to an existing structure. They replaced the load-bearing assumption that structure had always rested on.

Amplified rock had been getting louder throughout the 1960's, but it had never abandoned the blues inheritance beneath it. It never abandoned the belief that tension resolves and that the music builds toward something. That release is the point. Even the heaviest acts of the era retained that assumption. The upward motion was always there, promised and delivered. The system assumed release the way a sentence assumes a period. Sabbath removed the period. That single structural decision produced a consequence that would keep unfolding for decades.

The first consequence was the elevation of the riff to a position it had never previously held.

On Black Sabbath and Paranoid, songs don't build toward solos or climax in moments of individual ability. They orbit a repeating, down-tuned riff that everything else — bass, drums, vocals exist in service of. Guitar solos appear, but they don't define the songs. The riff defines the songs. That shift had structural implications that extended far beyond Sabbath themselves. Once riff weight becomes the core currency of heavy music, the terms of the arms race change entirely. Technical ability becomes optional. Structural gravity becomes mandatory. The evolutionary levers available to the next generation are speed, precision, and tonal density. All serve making the riff heavier, faster, or more extreme rather than making the soloist more impressive.

The second consequence was the normalization of minor tonality as foundation rather than device.

Before Sabbath, tritones and flattened fifths lived in rock harmony as passing tensions. The conflict that created momentary unease before resolving back into something stable. Tools for color, not structure. Sabbath made them the structure. The tritone wasn't a detour on the way to resolution. It was the destination. Once darkness is established as architecture rather than decoration, every band that follows has access to a tonal language that didn't exist as a legitimate option before 1970. The door opened and stayed open. Every subsequent mutation walked through it. The third consequence was the establishment of lyrical dread as a legitimate chronicle. "War Pigs" and "Electric Funeral" didn't approach their subject matter with irony, distance, or the theatrical wink that horror-adjacent rock had previously required to make darkness palatable. They addressed war, political corruption, and nuclear extinction with the directness of people who considered these genuine and immediate threats. Because they were. That sincerity created a template that proved remarkably durable. Heavy music could engage with real geopolitical crisis, with genuine fear, without softening it into metaphor or undercutting it with performance. The darkness was allowed to mean exactly what it said. Every band that subsequently used heavy music to address real world catastrophe inherited that permission directly from Sabbath's refusal to look away. Those three consequences didn't sit static. They became the conditions under which the next generation operated. Not as influences to acknowledge but as structural facts to build from. The riff was now currency. Minor tonality was now architecture. Lyrical dread was now a legitimate language. Any band that picked up a heavily amplified guitar after 1970 was working inside a space Sabbath had defined whether they knew it or not. Judas Priest arrived in the mid-1970's and did something precise with what Sabbath had built. They stripped the remaining blues traces from the framework entirely. Dual guitar precision replaced loose single-riff heaviness. The rhythm attack tightened. The distortion got cleaner but sharper with less doom, more precise. Priest didn't invent heaviness. They refined Sabbath's removal of swing into something with harder edges and faster attack. That refinement only makes sense as a next step because Sabbath had already proven that heaviness without blues resolution could sustain a commercial career. "Victim of Changes" demonstrates it precisely — the riff carries the same gravitational weight Sabbath established but the dual guitar attack gives it a cleaner, more surgical edge that Sabbath's doom architecture never sought.

Motörhead accelerated the entire frame. Tempo increased dramatically but the distortion stayed saturated and the riff remained dominant. Speed became a new kind of pressure — not the slow growth of dread Sabbath had pioneered, but a velocity that created its own overwhelming weight. The line from Sabbath's slowed gravity to Motörhead's overdriven velocity is direct and unbroken. The frame is the same. The stress test is different. "Overkill" does the opposite of Priest. The tempo is almost violent, the distortion maxed, but the riff is still the engine. Speed didn't replace the riff. It weaponized it.

The consequences were inevitable because of what happens to an audience once release is removed.

When music stops providing resolution, the listener doesn't disengage they acclimate. The tension that felt overwhelming on first exposure becomes the baseline on second. And once the baseline shifts, the previous level no longer delivers the same weight. The audience's tolerance for an unresolved tension rises, and the system must respond or become irrelevant. The options are limited. Either faster, heavier, more distorted, or more extreme. Within those parameters the pressure ladder is effectively without ceiling. Heavy music became a continuous escalation that musicians and audiences climbed together, each pushing the other further than either would have gone alone. That dynamic didn't require anyone to plan it. It simply followed from the removal of release as an option.

Hard rock was already fragmenting into multiple directions simultaneously. With progressive rock, glam, proto punk all emerging in the same period. The argument that metal might have merged through parallel channels regardless of Sabbath is worth examining. Heaviness was simply inevitable and Sabbath were one of several possible ignition points rather than the ignition point.

The continuity defeats that. Progressive rock pursued complexity and arrangement — it moved away from riff gravity. Glam pursued spectacle and sexuality — it retained blues swagger and added theater. Proto-punk deliberately reduced technical skill as an ideological statement — it was reacting against ability, not building a new kind of weight. None of these movements centered the down tuned riff as their primary structural identity. None of them removed blues resolution as a deliberate architectural choice. The direct lineage from Sabbath through the NWOBHM and into thrash shows a clear structural inheritance at every step. Creating riff dominance, minor tonality, and amplification weight with the refusal of release. That inheritance doesn't trace back to glam or progressive rock or proto punk. It traces back to four men from Birmingham in 1970. Without Sabbath, heaviness might have existed in fragments scattered across close genres. It would not have joined into a distinct and self-sustaining form.

If Sabbath had remained a niche act. If critics had successfully framed heavy minimalism as primitive and regressive. If labels had redirected investment toward progressive elegance the dominant evolution of 1970s rock tilts toward technical complexity rather than tonal mass. Heavy music might have existed, but as a sub-genre of hard blues rather than a self-sustaining system with its own internal logic and evolutionary momentum. A sub-genre is dependent on the form it lives inside. A separate system generates its own mutations, its own audience, its own future.

Commercial success at the scale Sabbath achieved doesn't just validate a sound. It locks the mutation in place. It tells every label, every promoter, every young musician watching from the outside that this is a viable direction. That the darkness isn't outlying. That the weight has an audience large enough to matter. Once that signal is sent it cannot be unsent.

After 1970, heaviness was no longer an experiment. It was a platform. And platforms don't stay static. They get built on. The speed came. The precision came. The extremity came. Each successive mutation had somewhere solid to stand because Sabbath had already proven that a music built entirely on unresolved dread could not only survive commercially but generate a lineage.

Sabbath didn't just respond to the collapse of optimism. They made every future form of extremity structurally possible. The culture ran out of ways to avoid darkness in 1970. It has been building on that darkness ever since.

Chapter 1 has covered the same ground from several angles deliberately. Optimism, economics, technology, audience, and the consequences. That repetition is not an oversight. Heavy metal did not emerge from a single cause. It emerged from the coming together of all of them at once and understanding that merging requires examining each pressure point on its own terms before the full weight of their collision becomes clear. If the argument has felt persistent, that is intentional.

CHAPTER TWO
When Heavy Scaled

Birmingham had honored the dread. The mutation had spread. And then the commercial infrastructure did what commercial infrastructures always do with forms that prove their viability. It absorbed them, scaled them, and in scaling them engineered away the volatility that had made them significant in the first place.

By the mid-1970's the heaviness that Sabbath had formalized alongside Zeppelin and Deep Purple had developed in parallel directions. It had been processed through the rock machine into something more comfortable than any of its source materials previously. The volume remained. The guitar heroics remained. The physical scale of the live performance remained. What had been engineered away was the confrontational edge. The quality of music that felt aimed at you rather than performed for you. It demanded engagement rather than offering spectacle at the safe distance that arena staging required. Heavy music had become a genre with conventions. A commercial pipeline that by the late 1970's those conventions had accumulated enough weight to be felt as constraints by the musicians who understood what the form was capable of and what it had traded away in becoming respectable.

Punk arrived in 1976 and demonstrated with brutal efficiency that the constraints were not inevitable. The distance between performer and audience was a choice. The technical hierarchy that arena rock had built was a convention, not a law. Music could be confrontational and immediate without the infrastructure of major label investment and arena touring that the existing commercial system had made seem indispensable. The punk lesson was structural rather than sonic. Not that heaviness was wrong, but that the infrastructure heaviness had built to sustain itself had reproduced the exact conditions of distance and comfort that heaviness had originally been a response to.

British heavy music absorbed the punk lesson without absorbing punk's sonic vocabulary. This is the NWOBHM's specific historical achievement. It took the energy, the directness, the DIY infrastructure logic, and the rejection of arena rock's comfortable distance. It applied all of it to a form of music that retained heaviness as its primary expressive tool. Not three chords and two minutes. Full heavy metal song architecture includes riffs, guitar solos, twin guitar harmonies, physical rhythm section weight. Then delivered with punk's urgency and punk's insistence that the relationship between band and audience should be immediate and real.

The geographic conditions that produced this synthesis were specific. Sheffield produced Def Leppard. Five teenagers whose early recordings carried the raw urgency of a band that had absorbed punk's energy without abandoning the heavy guitar vocabulary they had grown up with. The twin guitar work of Pete Willis and Steve Clark already demonstrated a harmonic sophistication and riff intelligence that the punk tradition had specifically excluded as ideological discipline. Newcastle produced Venom, whose contribution to the NWOBHM's legacy would extend far beyond the scene's commercial moment into the extreme underground's foundational files. London produced Iron Maiden, whose trajectory from the East End pub circuit to the global stage represents the most complete arc of the NWOBHM's development. This form found itself in small rooms discovering with a speed nobody had anticipated. The audience it had built there was significantly larger than those rooms could contain.

Judas Priest had been developing their synthesis of heaviness and precision since the early 1970s and by the late 1970s had refined it into a distinct contribution to the form's vocabulary. The twin guitar attack of Glenn Tipton and K.K. Downing operated with a harmonic intelligence and rhythmic precision that Sabbath's power-chord foundation hadn't required. Rob Halford's vocal range and operatic delivery gave the music an emotional register that extended the form's expressive capacity beyond what the blues-rooted vocal traditions of original heavy music had explored. Priest predated the NWOBHM generationally but Unleashed in the East in 1979 and British Steel in 1980 provided the technical and aesthetic template the younger bands were building in relation. The precision was the lesson. The twin guitar harmony was the inheritance. The understanding that heaviness could refine without being domesticated. That technical sophistication and confrontational aggression were not opposites and was NWOBHM's foundational premise. Priest had demonstrated it before the movement had a name.

Motörhead occupied the most structurally significant

position in the NWOBHM's ecosystem because they didn't fully belong. Lemmy's specific mixture of using his bass as a lead instrument with punk-influenced velocity sitting on top of a heavy rock foundation rooted in the same British tradition Sabbath had established. This made them the bridge figure the NWOBHM needed to justify its own creation. If Motörhead could be simultaneously the heaviest band in Britain and the most punk band in heavy metal, then the production the NWOBHM was attempting was not a contradiction. It was the logical next development of a tradition.

Overkill, Bomber, Ace of Spades — three records across 1979 and 1980. Each of these demonstrate the velocity and aggression that the NWOBHM was building its identity around. Lemmy didn't play bass like a bassist. He played it like a rhythm guitarist who had decided the low end was where the real argument was happening. The instrument cutting through the mix with a presence and aggression that redefined the rhythm section's function in heavy music. Thus giving subsequent practitioners, a template for how the bottom of the sonic spectrum could carry as much confrontational force as the guitar work above it.

Def Leppard's early recordings sit in this landscape with a tension that their trajectory would make legible in review. It wasn't yet visible in 1979. The Getcha Rocks Off EP and On Through the Night in 1980 carried NWOBHM's essential properties. Twin guitar work, physical rhythm section, vocal delivery without the melodic optimization that commercial ambition would later require. But the melodic intelligence was already present in the songwriting. The chorus architecture already showed a hook sensibility. The rest of the NWOBHM wasn't particularly interested in developing this. Def Leppard was a heavy band with a pop instinct they hadn't yet decided what to do with it. The decision, when it came, would take them further from the NWOBHM's infrastructure and closer to the commercial mainstream than any Sheffield contemporary. The producer who made it possible would define the sound of commercial heavy music for the decade that followed.

That story belongs to a later chapter. Here, in 1979 and 1980, Def Leppard were five Sheffield kids making heavy music with punk's urgency and metal's vocabulary. the same in their ambitions from the dozens of other young British bands discovering that the form they loved had more to offer than the arena rock machine had allowed them to express.

The second wave had found its form. The question was whether it had found its transportation.

THE INFRASTRUCTURE IS BUILT (1979-1982)

The music existed before the infrastructure did. This is always how it happens. The form develops in the available spaces, the rehearsal rooms and the pub backrooms and the small stages that any city contains. The specific infrastructure story of the NWOBHM is worth examining in detail because it established templates that the extreme underground would inherit and develop through the 1980's. As an example of the independent single, the specialist press, the dedicated venue as scene anchor, the direct relationship between the band and the audience without major label mediation. It demonstrates with unusual clarity how a musical movement builds its own commercial viability from the ground up when the existing commercial system has no mechanism for recognizing what it's dealing with. The major labels in 1979 were not looking at the NWOBHM. They were looking at punk's commercial moment, which had already peaked and was fragmenting into post-punk's various experiments. They set their eyes at the arena rock infrastructure that continued to generate reliable returns from established acts. The young British heavy bands emerging from Sheffield and Newcastle and London and Birmingham were not on the radar of any A&R department. There was no budget and infrastructure forethought to develop them on a commercial scale. Which meant they had to develop themselves. Press their own singles, book their own shows, build their own audience through the direct contact of the live circuit. They lacked the broadcast mediation of radio and television that the commercial system offered to the acts it chose to invest in.

The seven-inch single was the NWOBHM's primary medium of self-publication and its most significant innovation in the context of heavy music's history. Punk had established the independent seven-inch as a viable commercial object. The Buzzcocks' Spiral Scratch EP in 1977, self-released on the New Hormones label for a few hundred pounds, had demonstrated that a band could press its own recordings, distribute them through independent channels, and reach a meaningful audience without the major label infrastructure that the commercial system had always insisted was indispensable. The NWOBHM inherited that demonstration. They applied it to heavy music, pressing small runs of singles on independent labels. Neat Records in Newcastle, the bands' own imprints, the network of small regional labels that assembled around the scene with the specific energy that emerges when a form is developing faster than the existing commercial structure can absorb it.

The singles were raw. The production was minimal. The budgets were what the bands could assemble from their own resources and from the small labels' modest investment capacity. Nothing approaching the studio time and engineering that the major label system provided to its signed acts. The rawness was not a limitation in the context of what the music was trying to do. The NWOBHM's audience was not looking for the polished production of Arena rock's commercial standard. It was looking for the directness and the urgency that the arena machine had engineered away. The independent single's raw production was honest about its own conditions of production in exactly the way that the arena rock machine's polished product was not. The sound said: this was made with what we had, by people who wanted to make it badly enough to find a way to make it regardless of what the commercial system was willing to support.

Neal Kay's Bandwagon Heavy Metal Soundhouse in Kingsbury, north London was the scene's geographic anchor and its most important single institutional presence. A venue that functioned at the same time as a pub. A disco in the sense that Kay was operating as a DJ playing heavy records for an audience that had gathered specifically to hear them. A community space where the NWOBHM's developing identity was being defined through the direct interaction of the bands and their audience in a physical space. Both parties inhabited as equals rather than at the performer-audience distance that arena rock had institutionalized. Kay was not simply playing records. He was curating a scene and identifying the bands. The recordings that embodied the form's emerging identity. Giving them exposure to an audience that was already primed to receive them. Creating the feedback loop between the music and its community that every significant musical movement requires. They developed an identity rather than retaining a collection of individual bands making similar sounds in separate rooms.

Kay's relationship with Sounds magazine was the mechanism that took the scene from its London geographic anchor to a national audience. Sounds, one of the British weekly music press's significant titles alongside NME and Melody Maker. They occupied a more rock and metal-friendly editorial position than either of its competitors. They became the NWOBHM's primary critical infrastructure, the publication that named the movement, documented its development, and gave the bands and their audience a shared critical discourse through which the scene's identity could be debated and defined. Geoff Barton's coverage in Sounds gave the NWOBHM its name and its critical framework at the same time. The New Wave of British Heavy Metal as a label that acknowledged both the punk influence and the heavy metal foundation. This positioned the scene as a renewal of heavy music's essential properties rather than a departure away.

The Sounds coverage did something structurally significant beyond simply documenting the scene. It created a national map of a movement that had been developing s in multiple British cities without those cities being fully aware of each other's activity. A band in Sheffield, reading about a band in Newcastle in Sounds, understood that what they were doing was part of something larger than their local scene. That the blend they had arrived at independently was being arrived at independently by other bands in other cities/ This meant it was not a local accident but a structural development. A response to shared conditions that was producing similar music in separate places because the conditions rather than the specific influences were generating the form. That national awareness accelerated the scene's development in the same way that the tape trading network would accelerate the extreme underground's development a decade later. By making local mutations visible to geographically separated communities, it created the competitive awareness that drives rise and improvement.

EMI's signing of Iron Maiden in 1979 was the moment when the major label infrastructure acknowledged that the NWOBHM had built something commercially significant enough to warrant investment. The signing was not a discovery. Iron Maiden had already built a substantial live following through the pub and club circuit, had already released the The Soundhouse Tapes EP independently in 1979, had already demonstrated through their own infrastructure-building that the audience existed and was willing to pay to access the music. EMI was not creating the commercial opportunity. It was recognizing one that the band had already created through the NWOBHM's DIY infrastructure and decided that the major label system's distribution and promotion capacity could scale what the independent set-up had built.

The self-titled debut Iron Maiden in 1980 demonstrated what the major label investment added to what the DIY infrastructure had already established. They could provide production clarity that the independent singles' raw recording had not achieved. The distribution reaches that can put the record in shops across the country. The promotional support that generated radio play and press coverage beyond the specialist heavy music press that Sounds represented. The combination of the DIY infrastructure's audience and the major label's distribution and promotion capacity produced a commercial result that neither system could have achieved alone. This is the structural lesson of every underground movement's commercial breakthrough. The NWOBHM through thrash and grunge, and a lesson that the major label system has had to relearn with each successive movement. The system's logic always inclines it toward believing that it created the commercial opportunity rather than recognizing one that already existed.

Iron Maiden reached number four on the UK Albums Chart. Killers in 1981 reached number twelve. The Number of the Beast in 1982 reached number one. The trajectory is the argument. A band that had built its audience through NWOBHM's DIY infrastructure achieving commercial scale at a speed that the major label investment accelerated. It did not originate it; the infrastructure and the investment operated as a complementary system rather than competing.

Def Leppard's trajectory through the same period demonstrates the alternative path and its specific consequences. Iron Maiden's commercial breakthrough preserved the properties of the NWOBHM's sound. The twin guitar attack, the rhythm section's directness, the confrontational live energy that the pub circuit had developed. Def Leppard's commercial development involved a progression toward the melodic and production polish. Their specific songwriting intelligence had always been moving toward this. The signing to Phonogram in 1979 and the later recording of On Through the Night with producer Tom Allom represented the first step in a trajectory that would accelerate when the band encountered Mutt Lange.

Robert John "Mutt" Lange was not a heavy music producer in the sense that his background was rooted in the form's specific traditions. He was a producer of exceptional sophistication and commercial intelligence who understood how to build recordings of maximum emotional impact through the specific combination of arrangement clarity. A master of vocal production, and sonic density that FM radio and the emerging MTV infrastructure required. His work with AC/DC on Highway to Hell in 1979 demonstrated his capacity to preserve a heavy band's essential identity while delivering the production clarity that commercial radio demanded. His work with Def Leppard on High 'n' Dry in 1981 and Pyromania in 1983 would demonstrate something more consequential for the book's broader argument. NWOBHM's melodic intelligence, separated from the scene's DIY rawness and developed through Lange's production philosophy to its logical commercial conclusion, could produce heavy music of massive commercial scale.

Pyromania sold over ten million copies in the United States alone. The record that Def Leppard had arrived at by following their melodic instinct through the NWOBHM's infrastructure and out the other side into Lange's studio was not recognizably a NWOBHM record. The rawness was gone, the DIY urgency was gone, the confrontational honesty that the pub circuit had required was gone. What remained was the heaviness. The guitar density, the rhythm section's physical authority, the volume, and the distortion. All delivered through a production of unprecedented clarity and emotional impact that the commercial infrastructure could carry at a scale that it never been designed to achieve.

The thread that runs from Sheffield in 1979 to Pyromania in 1983 to Bruce Fairbairn's Sound City productions in the mid-1980's - is a single continuous argument about what happens when heavy music's intelligence encounters a philosophy designed for maximum commercial reach. Def Leppard was the first band to follow that argument to its conclusion. The conclusion defined the commercial sound of heavy music for a decade. The production philosophy that Lange developed was the direct ancestor of everything that a later Chapter traces through the hair metal era's engineering of broadcast-compatible heaviness.

NWOBHM's infrastructure had built something it hadn't

intended to build. Not just the scene's own commercial viability but the template for how heavy music's melodic potential could be developed toward commercial scale without abandoning the properties that made it heavy. The scene's bands followed that template all the way to its conclusion. Others stayed inside the infrastructure they had built and developed the form's heavier properties toward the escalation that the American thrash movement would inherit. Both paths were legitimate consequences of what the infrastructure had established. Both paths led somewhere significant. Neither path would have been available without the seven-inch singles and the Bandwagon Soundhouse and Neal Kay's curation and Sounds magazine's national map of movement. This assembled itself from the ground up because the existing commercial system hadn't been paying attention. The infrastructure had built the scene. The scene had built the future. And the future was about to cross the Atlantic.

WHAT IT EXPORTED 1980-1984)

The Atlantic crossing was not a single event. It was a transmission. A continuous, multi-directional, operation through the specific channels that music moves through when it travels between scenes with no direct commercial infrastructure connected. Records in import bins. Interviews in specialist press. Word of mouth between musicians who had heard something that recalibrated their understanding of what the form they were working in was capable of. The NWOBHM reached America the way all significant musical transmissions reach their destinations before the commercial infrastructure catches up. The dedicated attention of a small number of people understood what they were hearing and understood that it changed what was possible.

The American heavy music landscape in 1980 was not waiting for the NWOBHM. It had its own commercial infrastructure. The arena rock circuit, the FM radio format, the major label system's investment in established acts. Its own developing underground, the hardcore movement building its DIY infrastructure in the same years the NWOBHM was building its own. What the American landscape was missing was a model for how heaviness could be technically sophisticated and rhythmically aggressive. A rooting in the guitar-centered tradition without being domesticated by the arena rock machine or limited by hardcore's deliberate rejection of musical intricacy.

Metallica's particular debt to the NWOBHM is the most well-documented and most analytically significant example of the American impact. Both James Hetfield and Lars Ulrich didn't stumble upon the NWOBHM from outside. Ulrich was an early participant in the import culture that took overseas records here to American audiences before any domestic distribution existed to carry them. The teen Ulrich corresponding with British bands and tracking down independent singles with the obsessive concentration of someone that knew that the music he was consuming was a development of the form in which American heavy music had not yet developed. The Diamond Head connection is the most cited. Ulrich's sense for the Canterbury band's compositional sophistication. The riff-choreography of "Am I Evil," "The Prince" showing an architectural intelligence and an openness to materialize ideas musically over longer song lengths than the American heavy music scene had taken to on a similar level. Diamond Head were never commercially significant in the conventional sense. They built a cult following through the NWOBHM's infrastructure without achieving the major label breakthrough Iron Maiden's trajectory had demonstrated was possible. What contributed to the form's development was disproportionate to their commercial footprint. Which is the specific type of influence that analytical history must be careful to trace because the commercial record consistently underrepresents it. The bands that change what subsequent musicians understand to be possible are not always the bands that sell the most records. Sometimes they are the bands that a specific young drummer in California found in the import bin and played obsessively until the compositional logic had been fully absorbed and was ready to be expressed in a different context with different musicians and different ambitions.

The riff as extended compositional statement — not the two or four bar figures repeated as structural foundation but the developed musical idea moving through harmonic and rhythmic variations across the song's architecture. The specific inheritance Metallica drew from the most ambitious consultants. Kill 'Em All in 1983 carries this inheritance in its arrangement logic even where the sonic properties have been transformed by hardcore's velocity and aggression. The songs develop through multiple distinct sections with a compositional intention that hardcore's three-chord structure had specifically excluded. What arena rock had simplified into verse-chorus repetition. The NWOBHM's compositional sophistication and hardcore's velocity were the two source streams thrash synthesized. The synthesis was only possible because the NWOBHM had demonstrated that compositional and confrontational aggression were not mutually exclusive.

Iron Maiden's American breakthrough provided the commercial evidence that the transmission was not limited to underground influence channels. The Number of the Beast in 1982 achieved significant American sales and arena-level touring. Further demonstrating to the American infrastructure that British heavy music of technical sophistication could reach a mass audience without the melodic optimization FM radio had established as a commercial requirement. The twin guitar attack of Dave Murray and Adrian Smith, the compositional complexity of the arrangements, Steve Harris's bass-driven song structures. None of these properties had been softened for American consumption. The record was as uncompromising in its musical identity as anything the NWOBHM had produced, and it sold. That was the commercial proof the American arena rock infrastructure needed before it could acknowledge that the form it had been ignoring had built an audience it hadn't anticipated.

Bruce Dickinson's vocal performance deserves specific attention because it represents the NWOBHM's most complete development of the operatic tradition Rob Halford established. Where Halford had demonstrated that range and power with theatrical delivery were compatible with heavy music's identity. Dickinson demonstrated that those properties could be deployed with a narrative intelligence that made the vocal performance a compositional element rather than a display of technical capacity. The storytelling function of Dickinson's delivery — the specific way the vocal line carried lyrical content as narrative rather than statement. This gave Iron Maiden's recordings a dramatic coherence that distinguished them from every other form of heavy music. It proved enormously influential on the American bands building their own approaches in relation to the example.

Motörhead's American impact operated on a different axis. The velocity, the aggression, and the bass-forward sonic identity. Lemmy's development translated directly into the American hardcore and proto-thrash underground's understanding. An example of how fast heavy music could go while remaining rooted in the heavy rock tradition rather than departing into hardcore's minimal sonic palette. Ace of Spades reached American underground audiences through import channels and the tape trading networks beginning to develop in the early 1980's. It's a specific combination of velocity and heaviness as a direct influence on the tempo escalation thrash would use as its primary discriminator from everything that preceded it.

The export that mattered most was not any specific record or band but the demonstration the NWOBHM as a movement had produced. Heavy music could rebuild itself from the ground up through DIY infrastructure when the commercial system failed to develop it. That the form's technical and compositional potential was significantly greater than the arena rock machine. That the audience for technically sophisticated and aggressive heavy music was larger and more organically distributed than the existing commercial base had recognized.

That demonstration crossed the Atlantic and found the specific young musicians who were ready to receive it. The Bay Area thrash scene that produced Metallica and Slayer and Exodus and Testament was not the NWOBHM transplanted to California. It was the NWOBHM's transmission received by musicians operating in a different cultural context with different influences and different pressures. This developed into a form the NWOBHM itself had not anticipated and could not have produced. The hardcore influence the American scene brought to the production. the velocity escalation, the political directness, the specific aggression of the American underground's relationship to the Reagan era. This was not available to the British bands working in Birmingham, Sheffield, and London. The mixture required both source streams and the specific American conditions that made the combination possible.

Def Leppard's American trajectory completed a different version of the crossing with a different lesson embedded in its outcome. Pyromania in 1983 achieved its American breakthrough not through the underground transmission channels but through the commercial infrastructure's standard mechanisms. FM radio rotation, MTV video play, Arena touring support from a major label with sufficient investment to build the promotional and commercial success required. The record's American success was the commercial infrastructure's success as much as the bands. The recognition that melodic intelligence developed through Lange's production philosophy. It could satisfy FM radio's accessibility requirements while retaining the guitar density and rhythmic authority that distinguished it from the pop mainstream.

The lesson the commercial infrastructure derived from Pyromania's experience was not the lesson of the NWOBHM exporting two things at once. America received them as separate signals and built two separate futures from them.

The technical sophistication, the precision, the composition, the speed all fed the Bay Area thrash scene. Combined with hardcore's aggression, it produced the most significant heavy music mutation of the decade. The melodic intelligence and production ambition fed something else entirely: hair metal, the most commercially successful heavy music of the 1980s. Both were legitimate. Both grew directly from what the NWOBHM had built out of seven-inch singles, pub back rooms, Kay's curation, and Barton's national map. America took the second wave's form and split it into two streams running in opposite directions. The underground escalated. The mainstream optimized. Those streams would run parallel for a decade until they converged — and the collision produced the fragmentation that became heavy music's permanent condition. Birmingham started it. The NWOBHM carried it forward with new vocabulary, new infrastructure, and new ambition. What follows traces where those two streams went.

CHAPTER THREE

When Heavy Became Business

ARENA EXPANSION (1970–1976)

Heaviness didn't stay underground because nobody was listening. It stayed underground until somebody realized how much money was sitting there untouched. The moment that realization arrived, everything that made the music dangerous began negotiation with everything that makes an industry function.

Between 1970 and 1973, heaviness stopped being a risk anyone needed to take.

Before Paranoid charted, Black Sabbath were an experiment of dark, uncommercial, the kind of band that record labels tolerated rather than invested in. The moment the album hit number one, that calculation inverted. Labels saw numbers. Promoters saw ticket demand in cities that had never been part of the conversation. The amplified darkness had proven it could generate revenue, and revenue has a logic of its own. Once heaviness sells, it scales. And scaling doesn't just change the size of the operation. It changes the structure of the music itself.

The origin point matters. Black Sabbath began as Earth, playing Henry's Blues House. A rented space above a pub in Birmingham where capacity was measured in dozens rather than thousands. The walls were close. The volume was oppressive. Not as a performance choice but as a physical fact of the room. The audience wasn't watching from a distance and making judgments about the spectacle. They were inside the sound. No separation between source and listener. A pressure, shared equally by everyone in the room.

Arena expansion ended that relationship permanently. And for what replaced it was something the music was never designed.

By 1973, Led Zeppelin were filling Madison Square Garden. The touring infrastructure that had once meant a van, a driver, and a prayer was expanding into something that required coordination teams. The production managers, and budgets that would have been unrecognizable to the bands playing pubs back rooms three years earlier. PA systems scaled to fill stadiums. Lighting rigs grew tall enough to require structural engineers. The production itself became a statement before a note was played. The size of the stage told the audience something about the scale of what they were about to witness.

But scale introduced a problem nobody had fully anticipated. The music built for small rooms and built for suffocation, for the feeling of being physically trapped inside someone else's dread did not automatically translate across distance. In a club, slow dread works because the room enforces it. The walls hold the weight in. In an arena, the space swallow's subtlety whole. A riff that felt crushing at close range can dissolve into the upper tiers before it lands. Sonic mud that felt authentic at 800 capacity becomes a liability at 15,000 fans. The tempos had to tighten. The riffs had to sharpen. The choruses had to enlarge so the back row had something to grab. Heaviness didn't abandon its identity, it professionalized it. And professionalization always comes with a cost.

The distance between early Sabbath and the mid-1970's heavy sound is not a matter of taste. It is a matter of engineering.

Early Sabbath had loose swing buried beneath murky production with tempos that breathed unevenly, guitars that bled into each other, lyrics about paranoia and war delivered without theatrical polish or commercial consideration. It sounded like it was recorded by people who had never been told what a record was supposed to sound like. That rawness wasn't a limitation against which they were working. It was the truth of where they came from, captured without a filter.

By the mid-1970s, the filter was firmly in place. Recording budgets expanded. Studios upgraded to 24-track consoles that allowed producers to separate instruments with precision that earlier recording couldn't approach. The emphasis shifted toward clarity. With riffs that punched through FM radio compression, vocals that sat clearly above the mix, production that translated from a car stereo to an arena PA without losing its definition.

Judas Priest is the clearest example of what this pressure produced. They weren't alone in responding to it. Kiss took the same structural logic and pushed it to its furthest extreme. Where Priest engineered precision, Kiss engineered spectacle. The fire-breathing, platform boots, faces painted into icons that read from the back row of any arena on earth. The music itself was secondary to the delivery mechanism. By Alive! in 1975, Kiss had become a production company that also made records. The arena didn't just change their sound. It became their entire identity.

Priest stripped the remaining blues from the framework entirely — no swing, no looseness, no murk. Dual guitars locked into synchronized precision. Vocals controlled and deliberate. The leather and studs that became their visual identity weren't a fashion decision. They were a brand decision. An image that traveled across borders and demographics without requiring local context to decode them. That is not esthetic drift. That is structural adaptation to scale. Priest didn't stumble into their sound. They engineered it for the rooms they intended to fill.

The original mutation had solved a specific tension with optimism collapsing under the weight of industrial dread. Arena expansion created a new one, and it was in some ways more corrosive because it came from inside the music rather than from the culture surrounding it.

When a band moves from an 800-capacity hall to a 20,000-seat arena, the performer doesn't just get further away physically. They become a different kind of entity. Ticket prices rise to cover production costs. Security barriers appear between the stage and the crowd. Lighting rigs tower above the floor, turning the band into silhouettes against a wall of controlled spectacle. The audience that once pressed against the stage close enough to feel the amp heat, close enough to make eye contact — becomes a mass. Numbered seats. Designated sections. A crowd managed for efficiency rather than gathered for communion.

Heaviness got bigger. Connection thinned. And that thinning is not an emotional complaint, it is a structural reality built into the economics of scale.

As professionalism increased, risk decreased in precise proportion. Songs tightened into reliable shapes. Set lists standardized across cities so crew and production could execute without variables. Solos extended not because the music demanded it but because spectacle fills time and time fills venues. The distortion edges that once felt genuinely dangerous got cleaned up in the mix because clean distortion translates better to radio and protects the investment. The music had to function predictably to protect the revenue. The system made a trade of volatility for reliability. Danger for dependability.

And the youth noticed. Once the dread becomes an industry product that's well packaged, ticketed, barricaded, and broadcast on FM radio between car advertisements. It no longer feels like it belongs to them. It feels managed. Administered. Safe in the worst feasible way. The kids who needed the music to reflect something true about their lives found themselves watching it from the 40th row through a pair of binoculars.

By 1975 and 1976, arena rock dominance in the arena wasn't an emerging trend it was the established condition. Deep Purple, Led Zeppelin, and the bands that had followed in their commercial wake were operating at a scale that would have been incomprehensible to the scenes that produced them. Stadium tours normalized excess as a default. The distance between stage and floor had become both physical and symbolic. A gap measured not just in feet but in the cost of a ticket, the height of a barrier, and the number of people standing between a fan and the band they came to see.

The counterargument deserves a direct response. Bigger shows reach more people. Better production means better sound. More fans participating in the same cultural moment could be called a strengthening of the art form rather than a dilution of it.

But scale changes the feedback loop in a way that reach alone doesn't capture. In a small venue, the audience is part of the performance in real time. Their energy enters the room and the band responds to it, adjusts to it, is shaped by it in ways that can't be planned or replicated. In an arena, the band performs into lighting rigs and time codes. The event is scripted. Improvisation is a liability because mistakes cost money and money is now the organizing principle. The economic stakes don't just suppress volatility, but they make volatility actively dangerous to the business model.

Heavy music was born from instability. Industrial dread, cultural collapse, small rooms where anything could happen and sometimes did. The danger wasn't a marketing angle. It was the condition of the environment. When that environment gets replaced by a corporate touring circuit and when the dread gets scheduled, ticketed, and produced to specification — the tension that powered the original mutation doesn't disappear. It accumulates somewhere else. In someone younger. In a smaller room. In a city where the arena tour doesn't bother to stop.

If heavy music had remained club-based with moderate budgets, smaller circuits, no label investment beyond what the scene could sustain. The intimacy may have held considerably longer. The blues residue might never have been fully stripped. The professionalization that reshaped the sound for arena consumption might have arrived later, or not at all. The genre might have remained volatile, regional, and raw well into the late 1970's.

But that alternative required the labels to look at Paranoid hitting number one and decide not to act on it. That was never going to happen. Once heaviness proved it could move units at scale, investment followed with the inevitability of water finding a drain. Investment brought infrastructure. Infrastructure brought predictability. Predictability brought distance. And distance, for an audience that had chosen this music precisely because it felt close, honest, and dangerous, was a betrayal that accumulated quietly until it wasn't quiet anymore.

By 1976, the economic conditions that had produced the original mutation had returned to the streets the music came from. But the bands those streets had produced were arriving in private jets and leaving before the crowd had cleared the parking lot. The dread was still in the setlist. It just wasn't in the room anymore.

That gap didn't close on its own. It widened with every arena tour, every barricaded stage, every ticket price increase. And in the cities where the original sound had been born — in the streets that the private jets flew over without stopping — something was already beginning to form in response. It didn't have a name yet. But it had a direction.

The arena didn't just change the relationship between the band and the audience. It changed the relationship between music and the money behind it. And once money moves in at scale, it doesn't arrive quietly. It arrives with expectations — and those expectations reshape everything they touch.

LABEL INVESTMENT (1970–1976)

Once heaviness proved it could generate revenue on a scale, the money didn't knock. It walked straight in.

Between 1970 and 1973, the commercial evidence accumulated quickly. Paranoid topped the UK charts. Led Zeppelin were breaking attendance records across the United States. Albums the industry had treated as difficult and non-commercial were moving units in numbers that demanded a response. The labels stopped categorizing heavy bands as unstable experiments and started categorizing them as assets. As properties to be developed, protected, and optimized for return. The shift in language reflects the shift in relationships. An experiment can fail and be forgotten. An asset must be managed. And managed assets don't get to remain volatile.

That is the pressure this sub-chapter is built around. Not the music changing because musicians wanted it to. The music was changing because the money that now surrounded it had expectations and those expectations were structural, not esthetic.

The paper trail starts early. Sabbath's debut was recorded quickly, cheaply, and with minimal label interference. The rawness was partly intentional and partly a function of limited resources and limited expectations. By Master of Reality in 1971, the budgets were already higher. More studio time meant more layering, more deliberate construction, and more opportunity for producers and label representatives to have opinions about what the record should sound like. The sonic thickness that had originally been an accident of circumstance was becoming a managed aesthetic — something to be replicated reliably rather than stumbled upon.

Labels like Vertigo Records in the UK began positioning their heavy acts as flagship properties rather than fringe experiments. In the US, Warner Bros. poured money into distribution and coordinated radio pushes at a scale that independent promotion couldn't touch. FM rock radio was expanding rapidly across American cities in the early 1970s, and heavy albums were being sequenced and formatted to fit its requirements. The longer tracks structured around defined peaks, clearer hooks, singles isolated for rotation. "Paranoid" wasn't just a song. It was proof of concept that heaviness could produce a radio-friendly three-minute unit without losing its identity entirely. Once that proof existed, the planning cycles began. Release schedules. Marketing windows. Quarterly targets. The music was now operating inside a calendar.

FM radio didn't just distribute the music — it edited it. Program directors had slot requirements, and slot requirements had length limits, and length limits meant that songs which didn't conform got cut or didn't get played. The bands and labels that wanted rotation learned to build songs around those requirements before they entered the studio. The music was being shaped by broadcast infrastructure before it was even recorded. A quiet but profound reversal of the relationship between art and commerce that the original mutation had never had to negotiate.

Tour support budgets expanded in lockstep with recording investment. Album artwork shifted from abstract mood into deliberate branding with imagery designed to be recognizable across territories and demographics without requiring explanation. Release schedules tightened to maintain commercial momentum. The system developed expectations about output frequency, and those expectations were not requests. They were contractual.

The bands that signed into this system didn't do so naively. They did so because the alternative was obscurity. But the contract that solved the money problem created a different kind of trap. A band that had built its identity on having nothing to lose now had advances to recoup, schedules to meet, and a label infrastructure with opinions about everything from album sequencing to haircuts. The freedom that had produced the music was quietly exchanged for the security the music had earned. Most of them made that trade without fully understanding what they were giving up until the walls were already built around them.

The logic sits in a simple commercial reality. Once a genre stabilizes financially, the labels rationalize it — meaning they reduce its risk profile by identifying what works and optimizing its repetition. The sloppiness that once felt authentic began sounding unprofessional under higher fidelity recording conditions. Studios upgraded to 24-track consoles mid-decade, giving producers separation and clarity that earlier recordings couldn't achieve. Punch replaced murk. Definition replaced atmosphere. The investment didn't change what heavy music was trying to do. It changed the resolution at which it was allowed to do it.

Bad Company are the clearest product of this investment environment. Formed in 1973 from the wreckage of Free and Mott the Hoople — both raw, volatile, and commercially inconsistent — Bad Company were assembled with label infrastructure already in place and a clear commercial brief already understood. Their debut went platinum. The blues energy that Free had carried in its unpolished, unpredictable form got refined into something cleaner, more radio-ready, more dependable. The rawness didn't disappear entirely. It got optimized. That is what label investment does at scale. It doesn't kill the energy. It domesticates it. Bands that delivered clean, reproducible heaviness got promoted. Bands that remained volatile and difficult got managed toward compliance or dropped. The market selected for dependability, and the music that survived that selection looked and sounded markedly different from what had come before.

Scaled budgets carried scaled expectations. Advances had to be recouped. Tours had to hit revenue targets. Albums had to chart within windows that satisfied the label's quarterly logic. That financial pressure didn't encourage experimentation it actively discouraged it. Bands that had built their identity on volatility and risk now had accountants reviewing their decisions. The rational response to that environment isn't to push further into dangerous territory. It's to identify what worked last time and deliver a reliable version of it again. Heaviness became a code. A set of established signals that could be reproduced with confidence because the audience had already proven it would respond.

The instability this created was quieter than the one that produced the original mutation but no less real. Heavy music had felt dangerous in 1970 because it was genuinely uncontrolled. Nobody knew if it would work, nobody had mapped its boundaries, nobody had optimized it for any purpose beyond the need that produced it. By the mid-1970's it increasingly felt engineered. The danger was still in the lyrics and the volume, but it had been stress-assessed, quality-controlled, and approved for mass consumption. Youth audiences have an instinct for exactly this kind of displacement. They can feel the difference between music that was made because it had to exist and music that was made because the previous version sold well. When rebellion acquires obvious accountants, the rebellion stops being rebellion. It becomes a product with rebellion's face on the packaging.

The counterargument has genuine weight. Label investment provided better studios, better gear, and distribution infrastructure that independent scenes couldn't replicate. Without that capital, heavy music might have remained technically limited and geographically marginal. Powerful within its own borders but unable to cross them. The global reach that made heavy metal a genuinely international phenomenon required the kind of coordinated investment that only major labels could provide. That is real and it matters.

But investment carries a trade-off that compounds over time. The same infrastructure that expanded the music's reach also narrowed its acceptable range. Corporate filtering doesn't announce itself as censorship. It operates through incentive. The acts that delivered reliable returns got promoted. The acts that remained raw and unpredictable got pressure to conform or got dropped. Over several cycles of this selection process, the music that survived looked increasingly like what the market had already validated. The rawness didn't get banned. It got selected against, quietly and persistently, until the mainstream of heavy music reflected the preferences of the people funding it rather than the instincts of the people making it.

The investment strengthened the music's infrastructure. It also built the walls.

If labels had underinvested and treated heavy bands as niche acts — smaller budgets, limited distribution, no coordinated radio push. Metal might have remained regionally fragmented. The grime would have been preserved but the reach would have been limited. No arena tours. No global circuits. No unified heavy metal identity at all beyond just a collection of local scenes with overlapping instincts and no common infrastructure to bind them. The investment centralized the genre. It also concentrated on its contradictions.

By 1975 and 1976, the economic conditions that had originally produced heavy music had returned. Not to the arenas, not to the recording studios, not to the label offices where advances were being calculated. They returned to the streets. Youth unemployment spiked in the UK. The industrial cities that had generated the original dread were contracting again in ways that the music industry's quarterly reports didn't reflect and couldn't feel. The bands those cities had produced were now insulated from that contraction by the very infrastructure the labels had built around them. They were not protected by advances, tour revenues, and a commercial machine that had no interest in the economic conditions of the audience it was selling to.

That contradiction doesn't resolve quietly. When the music built from a specific kind of desperation becomes the property of corporations. When the rebellion gets a corporate address the need that produced it doesn't disappear. It relocates. It finds younger people in smaller rooms with cheaper gear and more immediate grievances. And it starts again from the beginning, this time with the added fury of feeling betrayed by the thing that was supposed to understand them.

TOURING CIRCUITS (1971–1976)

Heaviness proved it could fill rooms. Then it built a route between them.

Between 1971 and 1976, the touring infrastructure for heavy bands hardened from opportunistic travel into permanent, repeatable circuits. In the US, arena networks expanded beyond the major cities as smaller markets constructed venues to accommodate the scale of touring productions moving across the country. In the UK, university halls, civic centers, and sports arenas became reliable scheduled stops rather than one-off bookings. Promoters synchronized coast-to-coast schedules with a precision that turned what had once been volatile, unpredictable travel into a strategically mapped revenue flow. The road became a system. And systems have rules.

Once Sabbath and Zeppelin demonstrated that heavy acts could headline multi-thousand-capacity venues consistently and profitably, promoters standardized the routing. You didn't tour randomly anymore. You ran the circuits. The same cities, the same venues, the same sequence, season after season. The circuit wasn't just a map. It was a commitment to a particular kind of music delivered in a particular kind of way to a particular kind of audience that had already proven it would show up and pay. Deviation from that commitment was a financial risk the infrastructure wasn't designed to absorb.

Circuits change behavior in ways that accumulate slowly and become impossible to reverse.

When bands must deliver high-impact sets night after night across rooms holding thousands of people, variability becomes the enemy of the operation. Soundchecks stop being creative rehearsals and become technical confirmations. The same levels, the same positions, the same checks in the same order so the crew can move efficiently to the next city. Lighting cues lock in weeks before the tour begins. Set lists stabilize not because the band has stopped evolving but because the production has been built around specific songs in a specific sequence and changing that sequence costs time and money the schedule doesn't allow. Extended improvisation — the kind of open-ended exploration that had made early heavy music feel genuinely unpredictable becomes a liability when union crew curfews are written into the venue contract.

Heaviness tightens under repetition. It must.

Early Sabbath shows had felt genuinely unstable with the volume bleeding between instruments, tempos flexing under Ward's drumming, edges fraying in ways that felt less like sloppiness and more like the sound of something that hadn't been fully domesticated. That instability was part of what made the experience feel dangerous. Arena performance demanded something different. Songs had to land instantly for audiences sitting 200 feet from the stage with no guarantee of good sight lines. The riffs had to be percussive and immediate rather than slow and atmospheric. Open space decreased because open space at arena scale sounds like nothing rather than tension. Hooks enlarged because the back row needed something to hold onto.

Kiss rose directly within this structural requirement and took it further than any other band of the era. By Alive! in 1975, Kiss had built a touring operation that was less a rock show than a managed theatrical event. Fire-breathing. Blood-spitting. Pyrotechnics timed to the second. An image so standardized could be reproduced identically on a poster in Birmingham or a marquee in Chicago without a word of explanation. The music existed inside the delivery mechanism rather than the other way around. Kiss didn't just adapt to the circuit's requirements. They weaponized them by turning the repetition and scale the touring system demanded into the product itself. A Kiss show on night forty of a fifty-date run was identical to night one by design. The consistency wasn't a compromise. It was the point.

The physical infrastructure changed in parallel. Tour buses replaced vans not as a luxury upgrade but as a logistical necessity when distances between dates made overnight van travel impractical. Crew sizes grew from a handful of people who could load a van in twenty minutes to teams of specialists. Sound engineers, lighting technicians, stage managers, security personnel are each responsible for a specific component of a production too large for generalists to handle. Security barriers expanded from a rope at the front of the stage to physical structures designed to manage crowd pressure at scale. The front row stopped being handshake distance and became a guarded zone with its own protocols.

The logic is structural. Once ticket demand scales, logistics follow with mathematical certainty. Logistics require consistency because inconsistency introduces variables that cost money to resolve. Consistency reduces volatility. Reduced volatility eliminates the unpredictable moments that had made the music worth seeing in the first place.

Heavy music was born from instability. An industrial decay, cultural collapse, rooms where the volume was oppressive because the walls were too close and the band too loud for the space. The danger was environmental, built into the conditions before anyone played a note. Touring circuits converted that instability into a repeatable product with a consistent delivery mechanism and a predictable revenue outcome. The danger got engineered out because the danger was incompatible with the planning.

The instability that formed in response was no longer environmental. It was psychologically the slow accumulation of resentment in an audience that could feel the distance growing between themselves and the thing they had come to the show to be close to.

By 1975, the economic pressure that had produced the original mutation had returned to the streets. The touring machine had no mechanism for feeling it. The bands arrived, performed, and left. The production schedule didn't have room for anything else. Interaction was minimized by design. The audience that had once been inside the sound was now outside the barriers looking in.

Alienation returned but from the opposite direction. The original alienation had been the audience's response to a culture that refused to acknowledge their reality. This alienation was their response to a music that had once acknowledged it and then moved on without them.

The counterargument is that large tours expand access — more people get to see the bands, professional sound systems deliver a more powerful experience than a club PA ever could, and the circuits strengthen community by connecting audiences across cities who share the same musical identity. That is true and it matters.

But circuits centralized authority in ways that had consequences at ground level. Only label-backed acts with significant production budgets could afford sustained runs on the major circuits. Smaller, rawer bands. The kind that carried the volatility the arena system had processed out of the mainstream couldn't compete with the production scale audiences. The entry barrier rose with every production upgrade. The ladder became steep enough that most people couldn't reach the first rung.

A young band in Birmingham or Leeds in 1975 playing the same venue Sabbath had used as a rehearsal space five years earlier watched a national touring package roll through their city with its own support acts already contracted. Its own production crew, its own barricades. The venue that had been their room was now a stop on someone else's circuit. The local identity that had made the music meaningful in that specific place had been displaced by something that looked the same in every city it visited.

If touring had remained fragmented — regional halls, inconsistent routing, no national circuit infrastructure — heavy music might have preserved its local character longer. Distinct scenes would have developed with their own identities, their own sounds, their own relationship to the audiences that produced them. The genre might have remained unstable and diverse rather than unified and scalable. Much less powerful as a commercial entity but more honest as a cultural one.

Instead, the circuits unified heaviness into a class system. Headliners dominated arenas. Openers competed for exposure slots. Local acts got displaced by national packages that arrived with their own support already contracted.

Economic efficiency overrode local volatility at every level because local volatility didn't translate into reliable ticket sales across fifty cities. The circuit rewarded what it could replicate and discarded what it couldn't.

That pressure accumulated at ground level in exactly the cities where the original music had been made. By 1976, younger bands in London and New York were beginning to reject scale itself. Not because they lacked ambition but because scale had become synonymous with distance, and distance was the thing against which they were reacting. Smaller rooms. Faster sets. Shorter songs. Minimal gear. The deliberate inverse of everything the arena circuit had optimized. Not a lack of resources but a rejection of what the resources had produced.

Touring circuits solved profitability and reach. In doing so they created a structural gap between the stage and the street that the original music had been built to eliminate. The room-level friction that had made heavy music dangerous had been systematically removed by the same infrastructure that had made the music globally accessible.

The system had stabilized. And stability, in the history of this music, has always been the thing that makes the next rupture inevitable.

But the rupture wasn't only about distance between a stage and a crowd. It was about something the circuits had done to the music itself. Something harder to name but impossible to ignore once you heard it. The music that had come from specific places, which had carried the sound of those places inside it, was starting to sound like it came from nowhere at all. And nowhere, it turns out, is an extremely dangerous place to build a culture.

GEOGRAPHIC HOMOGENIZATION (1971–1976)

Listen to the opening riff of "Black Sabbath" and you are standing in Birmingham. Not metaphorically — literally. The weight of it, the slowness, the refusal to resolve. These are not compositional decisions made in the abstract. They are the sound of a specific place at a specific moment pressing itself into the music through the people who lived there. You could not have made that record in Los Angeles. Geography is in the grain.

Before the circuits hardened and the routing standardized, heavy music carried its location inside it the way a person carries an accent. Sabbath sounded like Birmingham. An industrial, gray, slow, and oppressive in the way that a city built on factory labor and wartime damage is slow and oppressive. Early American hard rock carried the blues geography of its regional circuits. The Detroit aggression of the MC5, the Southern weight of early Lynyrd Skynyrd, sounds that could only have come from the specific tension of the specific places that produced them. The music reflected its environment because the bands were still physically rooted in those environments. The local accent was intact.

Between 1971 and 1976, the circuits erased it.

National touring patterns and major-label distribution flattened the accent with an efficiency that wasn't malicious. It was simply the logic of scale applied to culture. A band that wanted to headline circuits across the UK and the US had to translate. Same set. Same sound. Same impact in London, New York, Chicago, and Los Angeles. That requirement restructures music from the inside out.

If the riff spacing is too murky, it won't cut through the reverb of a 15,000-seat arena in Chicago. If the tempo drags too heavily, Los Angeles radio program directors won't add it to rotation. If the image is too specifically tied to a regional identity — too Birmingham, too Detroit, too rooted in a particular street-level reality then the press in cities that don't share that reality won't know how to market it and won't bother trying. So, the bands that wanted to survive at scale made adjustments. The production sharpened. The midrange tightened. Song lengths normalized around radio-friendly durations. Choruses enlarged to give arena audiences something universal to grab on to. The local accent softened. The regional specificity that had made the music feel like it belonged to a particular place got sanded down into something that could belong to everyone. Which is another way of saying it belonged to no one in particular anymore.

This wasn't simply about money. It was about the requirements of consistency at scale. A touring circuit running shows across dozens of cities needs a product that works in all of them. Not a product that works brilliantly in one city and adequately in the rest, but a product engineered for universal delivery. Heavy music needed to be able to walk into a room full of strangers and be immediately understood. That requirement doesn't kill variety. It kills specificity. And specificity was the thing that had made the music feel true.

AC/DC makes the geographic argument most concretely. Formed in Sydney in 1973, they carried an Australian working-class identity as specific and rooted as anything Birmingham had produced — raw, direct, built on the same kind of industrial labor culture that had generated Sabbath's dread. But the international circuit had no mechanism for Australian specificity. To cross into the UK and US markets, the edges had to be managed. The accent remained. Bon Scott's delivery was irreducibly his own but the production cleaned up, the image standardized into something universally readable, and the Australian-ness that had saturated their earliest recordings became a flavor rather than a foundation. By the time High Voltage reached international release in 1976, AC/DC sounded like they could have come from anywhere that was loud, young, and angry. Which was precisely what the circuit required.

The same compression happened on the American side. The MC5's Detroit aggression as raw, political, rooted in the specific fury of a city burning through its own contradictions got processed out of the mainstream as the circuits standardized. Lynyrd Skynyrd's Southern weight survived longer because it had been romanticized into a marketable identity. Even if that identity became a costume rather than a condition once the arena circuit got hold of it. The American regional accents didn't disappear entirely. They became genre markers. Safely contained, reliably reproducible, stripped of the specific urgency that had made them matter in the first place.

The logic follows from the circuit itself. Once touring

infrastructure unifies cities into a single commercial network, survival at the national level requires removing whatever doesn't translate across that network. The friction that made the music specific is the same friction that makes it difficult to scale. So, the friction gets removed. Not violently, not with any awareness that something important is being lost, just quietly and incrementally, each compromise made for a good practical reason until the accumulation of good practical reasons has produced something that no longer sounds like anywhere.

Early Sabbath's atmosphere worked because it was genuinely new and genuinely specific. Nobody had heard that particular weight before, and the specificity was part of what made it powerful. By 1974 and 1975, clarity won because clarity scaled and specificity didn't. The instability this produced was quiet at first. When the local flavor erodes gradually, the audience doesn't register a single moment of loss. They register a slow accumulation of distance. The music gets bigger. The production gets more impressive. But somewhere in that growth, the youth in specific cities stop hearing themselves in it. Heaviness becomes placeless. It feels imported rather than grown, delivered rather than generated. The sound might be massive. But it is no longer theirs. And music that is no longer yours is just noise at high volume.

The counterargument is that cross-city touring doesn't erase regional character. Those scenes continued to exist and thrive throughout the 1970s, that Detroit, New York, and London all maintained distinct rock cultures the arena circuit didn't absorb or eliminate. That is accurate. Regional scenes did persist. Local identities did survive below the waterline of the mainstream.

But the pressure being described here operated at the top tier. At the level of the arena circuit, the major label, the FM radio playlist, and the international press. At that level, the dominant heavy sound converged on a template that could function universally, and the more successful a band became within that system, the less geographically specific it could afford to remain. The regional character that survived did so in the spaces the mainstream didn't bother to occupy. In the smaller venues, the independent labels, the scenes that hadn't yet attracted the commercial attention that would have required them to generalize. Those spaces were important. They were also, increasingly, where the next rupture was being assembled.

If touring circuits had remained regionally segmented with smaller routes, city-specific scenes developing without the pressure of national standardization — heavy music might have splintered into distinct urban dialects much earlier. A Birmingham strain defined by industrial weight. A New York strain carrying a different kind of urban aggression. A West Coast strain shaped by entirely different social conditions. No unified heavy metal identity, just a collection of local forms with overlapping instincts and no shared commercial infrastructure to flatten the differences between them. Diverse, volatile, and rooted. Less powerful at scale, but more honest about where it came from.

Instead, homogenization unified heaviness into a transferable product. In doing so created fractures that would define the second half of the decade. By 1976, young musicians in London and New York were reacting not just to the excess of corporate scale but to the uniformity it had produced. They wanted something immediately. Something local. Something that sounded like the specific street they were standing on rather than a sound engineered to work on every street equally. The reaction wasn't only about volume or speed or the rejection of guitar solos. It was about reclaiming specificity while demanding that music sound like it came from somewhere real, made by people for whom that somewhere was still the whole world.

When heaviness had to sound identical in London and Los Angeles, it stopped sounding like anywhere. And once music loses its sense of place, the people who needed it to have one will build something new to replace it. Something smaller, rawer, and angrier for the loss.

The loss wasn't abstract. It was the specific experience of being a young person in Birmingham or Detroit or Leeds in 1976, putting on a record that was supposed to speak for you, and hearing something that spoke for everyone in general and no one in particular. That gap between the music that had once felt like yours and the music that now felt like a product with your face on the marketing is not a critical complaint. It is the precise feeling that makes people pick up instruments and start again from scratch.

But the geographic flattening didn't happen in isolation. The circuits homogenized the live experience. The labels homogenized the recorded one. And running alongside both while reinforcing every compression, validating every compromise, circulating the same handful of names until they became the only names was a media infrastructure that had developed its own definition of what heavy music was supposed to sound like. Once the press and the radio agreed on that definition, deviation didn't just become commercially risky. It became invisible.

MEDIA STANDARDIZATION (1972–1976)

Touring unified the stage. The media unified the narrative.

By the early 1970s, FM radio had displaced AM as the dominant rock distribution channel across the United States. The shift wasn't just technical, it was cultural. FM's broader frequency range allowed higher fidelity reproduction, which made it the natural home for the dense, layered rock production heavy music was developing toward. Program directors-built playlists around the proven acts, the ones whose sales had already demonstrated that their audience would follow them to the dial. Album-Oriented Rock — AOR — emerged as the dominant format, and AOR had requirements. Clear production. Strong hooks. Defined track lengths that fit the programming slot without requiring a judgment call. If the music didn't fit the slot, it didn't get rotated. And if it didn't get rotation, it didn't exist at scale no matter how powerful it was in a room.

Boston's 1976 debut makes the mechanics of this visible with unusual clarity. The album was built in a home studio by Tom Scholz over several years, engineered from the beginning around FM radio's specific frequency response and dynamic range requirements. The guitars were layered to fill the stereo field without muddying the midrange that FM compression would emphasize. The vocals sat precisely where a car stereo would reproduce them most clearly. The songs peaked at moments calculated to work within programming slots. The result was an album that sounded enormous on radio because it had been designed for radio before it was designed for anything else. The format was the production brief. That reversal — from music shaped by necessity to music shaped by broadcast infrastructure — is the clearest illustration of what AOR did to the relationship between creation and distribution.

The trade press sped up the compression from a distinct perspective but to the same end. Publications like Creem in the US and Melody Maker and Sounds in the UK were not just writing about heavy music — they were creating a sense of what it was. Every review that articulated the prevailing heavy sound in certain terms — loud, precise, leather-clad, riff-driven, arena-ready — threw another brick into a wall that bands either had to occupy or exist outside of. Critics did not intend to confine the music. They wanted to describe it, define it, to make it legible to readers who wanted a map of the landscape. But description at scale turns prescription. Once enough critics in enough publications came together to agree on what heavy music sounded like, the consensus came directly back to the decisions of labels, producers, and bands. That description became the template. It became the template and that was the expectation. The expectation became the filter that turned out recent music — and anything that didn't filter smoothly just got filed under difficult, uncommercial or just ignored. Media is not just about mutation. It stabilizes it — and stabilization is the start of calcification. Once the FM playlists, the cover stories and the transatlantic press cycles came together under a constricted description of what heaviness needed to sound like, experimentation ceased having the formality of evolution and became error. A band that strayed too far from that well-trodden path didn't get looked upon as a pioneering one, it instead got reviewed as confused or self-indulgent or simply not covered at all. That flattening accelerated not because bands purposefully adopted sameness but rather deviation meant reduced visibility, and decreased visibility in the commercial system is simply equivalent to no existence. The reasonable response for a band with accruals to recoup and tour slots to fill was to remain legible. To provide what the format recognized. To be Heavy as in the exact way that the media had described it. This is a different kind of pressure from what the touring circuits or the label investment formed. Those pressures worked through economics. Direct impacts of financial choices. Media pressure worked through a narrative. It controlled what was possible to describe, determining what was possible to imagine. If the vocabulary that was available to speak about heavy music only included words that fell under an established template, then music that did not fit that template contained no language in which it could be understood. It was outside of the conversation. And outside the conversation, to most of the audience, meant outside the world. The international press cycles reinforced the same handful of names until those names became synonymous with the form itself. Repetition built recognition. Recognition built expectation. Expectation built a standard. Once a standard exists, anything that falls short of it is a failure and anything that exceeds it in the wrong direction is a threat. The youth resistance that had originally made heavy music necessary was now being processed through a media infrastructure that had defined what that resistance was allowed to look like.

Because if the media can explain you, package you, and circulate you predictably. You are no longer dangerous. You are a genre. And genres have rules.

The counterargument is that media coverage didn't constrain heavy music. It built it. Without Creem and Melody Maker running cover stories, without FM radio delivering albums into living rooms across America and Britain, heavy music remains a regional phenomenon with a devoted but limited audience. The press gave the music critical language. That language created communities of people who could recognize each other across geographic distance. Fans in rural Ohio who had never been to a concert but knew every track on Paranoid because a radio station in Cleveland had put it in rotation. The media didn't cage the music. It carried it.

That is true and it matters. But carrying something and defining it are two different operations, and the press did both simultaneously. The coverage that built the audience also built the walls. Every article that described the definitive heavy sound in specific terms added to a consensus that bands had to navigate whether they wanted to or not. The audience that FM radio created was real and large and genuinely passionate. It was also an audience that had been taught what to expect and audiences that know what to expect are harder to surprise, harder to push, and quicker to reject music that doesn't deliver the familiar signals. The media built the community. It also trained the community's expectations in ways that made experimentation progressively more difficult to sustain commercially.

If media coverage had remained fragmented — regional press with no transatlantic coordination, FM radio without AOR format standardization, no unified critical vocabulary developing around a narrow definition of heaviness — the music might have evolved in multiple directions simultaneously without any single template achieving dominance. Stranger, more experimental forms of heavy music might have found audiences in the gaps between markets. The definition of what counted as heavy might have remained contested and alive rather than settled and enforced. The compression that produced the rupture might have been delayed or might have produced a different kind of rupture entirely.

Instead, the media infrastructure converged on a definition at precisely the moment when the other pressures — arena expansion, label investment, touring circuits, geographic homogenization — were converging on the same point from different directions. The narrative pressure didn't cause homogenization alone. It completed it. It gave homogenization a language, circulated that language internationally, and made it the only language available for talking about the form. By the time the rupture came, it wasn't reacting to any single pressure. It was reacting to all of them simultaneously. To the full weight of a system that had taken something volatile and dangerous and made it entirely, suffocatingly legible.

By 1976, the system that had grown from Sabbath's debut was operating at a scale that would have been unrecognizable to the people who built it. The arenas were full. The labels were profitable. The circuits were running. The press was covering the same names in the same language in publications on both sides of the Atlantic. Heavy music has achieved everything that commercial success is supposed to achieve — reach, stability, infrastructure, identity.

And it had lost the thing that made it necessary.

The young people standing outside that system in 1976 in London bedsits, in New York lofts, in the cities the arena tours flew over without stopping. Weren't reacting to the music itself. They were reacting to what the music had become. To the distance. Regarding the ticket prices. To the leather that had stopped being a working-class uniform and become a costume. To the dread that had been scheduled, produced, and delivered on time every eighteen months with a marketing campaign attached. To the specific suffocation of watching something that had once spoken for you get translated into a language that spoke for everyone and therefore spoke for no one.

Punk didn't emerge from nowhere. It emerged from the

precise gap between what heavy music had promised and what the system had made of that promise. It was smaller, faster, cheaper, and angrier — not because those were aesthetic preferences but because every one of those qualities was the direct inverse of what the arena circuit had optimized for. The rejection was architectural. It was a generation dismantling the structure that had been built in their name and rebuilding it from the floor up with the materials they could afford. The system had scaled. The margins had broken. And the next mutation was already in the room.

Chapter 3 has gone through five pressures — arena expansion, label investment, touring circuits, geographic homogenization, media standardization — and the discussion has been designed to be cumulative. Because no pressure led to the events described, each subchapter has looked at the same period from a different angle. The scaling of heaviness was not due to any one decision, contract, tour, or radio format. Because of all of them that worked together at once, each system strengthening the other, finally, the combined system weight forced the rupture that the last subchapter explains. The punk argument in this chapter closing chapter is not an epilogue. It's the product of everything else that comes before it — the point at which all the straining pressure comes loose. Punk didn't come about because musicians were lazy or angry or bored. It was produced because the system heavy music erected had left a structural gap that the system itself had no way to repair. The gap between the stage and the street. Between the record and the room from which it originated. Between the dread of that lyric and the solace of a private jet. Punk stepped into that gap and was named for it. Chapter 4 will investigate the rupture itself — its internal logic, its structural corrections, and the instability

for it. Chapter 4 will investigate the rupture itself — its internal logic, its structural corrections, and the instability

CHAPTER FOUR
When Punk Rewrote the Rules

ACCESS OVER SKILL (1974–1977)

By 1975, heavy music had built a ladder. It just hadn't told anyone how steep it had become.

The professionalization that arena expansion demanded had produced a technical hierarchy that operated as efficiently as any entry barrier the music industry had ever constructed. Dual-guitar harmonies that are locked into synchronized precision. Extended solos running four, five, six minutes. Not because the song required it but because the arena did, because spectacle fills distance and distance had become the defining condition of the live experience. Clean execution under massive PA systems that exposed every hesitation, every missed entry, every moment of uncertainty that a club environment would have absorbed into the noise. Large tours ran on rehearsal discipline because mistakes cost money and money was now the organizing principle of the entire operation. Judas Priest by 1975 represented the endpoint of this trajectory. An act so thoroughly engineered for precision delivery that impulse had been removed not as a loss but as a liability.

Skill had become currency. And currency, by definition, is something not everyone has.

At the same time, the economic floor was dropping out from under the generation that had grown up with heavy music as its inheritance.

In the UK, the IMF crisis of 1976 arrived as the visible confirmation of what youth unemployment statistics had been suggesting for two years. The postwar promise of stable industrial work had not just stalled but collapsed. In the US, urban decay had hollowed out cities with a thoroughness that made the word decline feel hopeless. New York City in 1975 was functionally bankrupt. The South Bronx was burning. Cheap space existed in abundance because nobody with options wanted to be there. What didn't exist was money for rehearsal rooms, quality gear, recording time, or the kind of sustained practice that arena-level precision required. The base of serious musicianship had a cost, and the cost had become unaffordable for the generation most likely to need it.

The tension this created was structural and it was suffocating. On one side: music that had organized itself into a technically demanding, professionally administered, media validated hierarchy that required years of development to enter. On the other: a generation with energy, anger, and genuine need for musical expression and no economic pathway into the system that had claimed ownership of the form. The message the mainstream sent, without intending to and without caring about the response, was explicit. To participate, you must first qualify. Qualification takes time and money. Time and money are exactly what you don't have.

Mutation answers exclusion. It always has.

In the summer of 1974, the Ramones began playing CBGB on Bowery Street in lower Manhattan. A room that seated perhaps 300 people on a good night and smelled of stale beer. Decades of accumulated grime. It had a stage so small that the distance between the band and the front row was measured in inches rather than feet. No barricades. No production crew. No distance.

What there was: four kids from Queens playing songs that lasted under two minutes, built on three or four chords, delivered at speed with a locked rhythmic precision that had nothing to do with blues influence or progressive structure or any of the sonic vocabulary that arena metal had established as the definition of serious musicianship. No extended solos. No dynamic builds. No mythic dread accumulating over seven minutes of distinctive tension. Just downstroke after downstroke, song after song, the set over before an arena audience would have finished finding their seats.

In London, the Sex Pistols detonated the same principle with a different accent. Three chords. Confrontational delivery that had no interest in technical display because technical display was the enemy. It was the thing that separated the performer from the audience and declared that only certain people were qualified to stand on the stage. Short sets. Hostile energy directed not outward at some abstract darkness but inward at the room. At the industry, at the system that had decided who got to make music and who got to watch.

This was not inability. That point cannot be overstated and the counterargument that raises it needs to be killed cleanly before it gains traction. The Ramones played with a rhythmic precision that most arena bands couldn't replicate at that tempo. The locked downstroke attack of Tommy Ramone's drumming and Johnny Ramone's guitar required as much discipline as any dual-guitar harmony Judas Priest had engineered. It is discipline of a different and deliberately unglamorous kind. The Sex Pistols were managed, styled, and strategically confrontational in ways that required sizable intelligence to sustain. Malcolm McLaren understood exactly what he was building and why. The reduction was a choice. The minimalism was ideology. They chose three chords not because they didn't know there were more but because three chords were enough — and enough was the argument.

It was not inability. It was refusal.

Three chords eliminate hierarchy because hierarchy requires complexity to justify itself. If the music only needs three chords and anyone can learn three chords in an afternoon, the gatekeeping infrastructure that arena metal had spent five years constructing becomes irrelevant overnight. Short songs eliminate indulgence. The extended solo, the dynamic build, the seven-minute atmospheric construction. Because indulgence is a luxury that requires both the technical ability to sustain it and an audience with the patience to receive it. Punk music had no interest in refining either. The absence of solos removed the moment in every arena metal song. Where one person stepped forward and declared themselves more qualified than everyone else in the room. Minimal gear reduced the economic barrier to participation. Not free. Not easy. But possible in a way that a 24-track studio session and a 50-date arena tour were not possible.

Punk restructured participation. That is the precise and complete description of what it did. Not the sound. Not the image. Not the attitude. The structure of who was allowed to make music and under what conditions.

Predictability follows directly from the pressure. Once heaviness became ordered and technically demanding, once the ladder had been built high enough that most people couldn't reach the first rung, a generation locked out of that system had exactly two options. Train for years and accumulate the technical skills the system demanded. Find the money for proper gear and rehearsal space and recording time. Then hope that the industry notices and enters the hierarchy on its own terms. Or reject the ladder entirely and build something that didn't require one. Under economic pressure, rejection is faster. Under the specific economic pressure of 1975 and 1976 in London and New York, rejection was the only option that didn't require resources nobody had.

The structural traits of punk maps are so precisely on the pressures that produced them that the relationship stops looking like a coincidence and starts looking like engineering. Which is exactly what it was, even if the engineers didn't think of themselves that way. Short songs reduced rehearsal overhead and maximized immediacy in venues where attention was finite and competition for it intense. The absence of solos removed the virtuoso gatekeeping that had made arena metal feel like a credential-based profession. Fast tempos compressed maximum energy into minimum time. The opposite of the arena metal economy where more time meant more spectacles thus equaling more revenue. Minimal gear reduced the economic barrier to entry from a number that required label investment to a number that required a part-time job and a pawnshop.

This mutation doesn't reject heaviness. It rejects permission. The dread is still there in speed, the aggression, the refusal to resolve anything neatly. The darkness is still there in the lyrics, the confrontation, the refusal of comfort. What's gone is the requirement that you earn the right to express it. Punk said the darkness belongs to anyone who feels it. You don't need to qualify. You don't need to ask.

If arena heavy had remained accessible. If ticket prices had stayed within reach of the audience, the music had originally claimed as its own. If the venues had stayed small enough to maintain the physical closeness that made the experience feel dangerous rather than administered. If the performance structures had remained loose enough to accommodate impulse the rupture might never have reached the force it did. Youth frustrated with the technical hierarchy might have filtered gradually into the existing circuits. Finding ways to participate within the system rather than building a parallel one outside it. The ladder might have stayed low enough that climbing it remained a reasonable aspiration rather than a generational impossibility.

Instead, scale hardened the walls with every arena tour, every production upgrade, every ticket price increase. The ladder got taller. The entry cost got higher. The distance between the stage and the street got wider. And the generation standing outside that system ran out of patience at precisely the moment they ran out of economic options.

Punk tore the walls down. Not metaphorically — structurally. The three-chord vocabulary, the two-minute song, the fifty-capacity venue, the photocopied flyer, the self-booked show. Each one was a specific dismantling of a specific wall that the arena system had constructed. The demolition was precise because the frustration was precise. They knew exactly what they were tearing down because they had been standing outside it long enough to memorize every brick.

Once access replaces skill as the primary currency, the consequences accumulate faster than the system can respond to them. Anyone can start a band. Local identity returns because local identity is all that's required. You don't need to be legible to Chicago and Los Angeles at the same time, you just need to matter on your own block. Small venues regain relevance because small venues are where the music was always most honest. Sound becomes raw again not because loyalty is technically impossible but because polish is now politically suspect. Because polish is what the other side uses, because polish is the sound of distance and distance is exactly what this music exists to eliminate.

Punk doesn't evolve from nowhere. It is the system correcting for over-professionalization with the same logic that produced the over-professionalization in the first place. Heavy music scaled because the pressure to scale was irresistible. Punk ruptured because the pressure to rupture was equally irresistible. The mutation wasn't a choice any more than the original heaviness was a choice. It was the inevitable response of a generation that had been told it needed permission — and had decided, with considerable force and little patience, that it didn't.

Not because they couldn't play. Because they refused to ask.

SCENE OVER CIRCUIT (1975–1978)

Touring circuits unified the map. Scenes fracture it back into something human.

By 1975, heavy music moved through national grids with the efficiency of an organization operation. Because that is precisely what it had become. Promoters routed the same headliners through the same arenas in the same sequence season after season. Major labels coordinated press campaigns, radio pushes, and ticket sales across cities with a precision that left nothing to chance and little to impulse. The circuit was a machine, and the machine had one requirement: fit the format or don't participate. If you weren't signed you weren't routed. If you weren't routed, you weren't visible. If you weren't visible you didn't exist at the level where the music was being defined, distributed, and consumed by the audiences large enough to matter commercially.

That is structural control at its most complete. A system so thoroughly optimized for its own keeping that it had lost the ability to recognize anything outside itself as music worth hearing.

At the same time, the cities the arena circuit flew over without stopping were generating exactly the conditions that produce parallel foundation. Youth unemployment in Britain was climbing toward figures that made the postwar social contract look like a broken promise rather than a temporary setback. In New York, urban decline had created something inconsistent — a city so economically devastated that cheap space was everywhere, but so disconnected from the industry's commercial infrastructure that cheap space was all there was. No A&R attention. No label scouts. No national press coverage. Just empty rooms and people with nowhere else to be.

Mutation answered by abandoning the grid entirely. Not retreating from it, not negotiating with it, not waiting for it to lower its barriers. Abandoning it as irrelevant to the actual project of making music in a specific place for a specific audience standing right there in the room.

CBGB became the fixed node around which the New York scene organized itself. Not because it was chosen strategically but because it was available, affordable, and willing to book bands that no circuit promoter would have returned a phone call. Bands didn't wait for national tours to validate their existence. They built weekly residences. The same room, the same audience rotating and expanding through word of mouth. The same bills cycling through the Ramones, Television, Blondie, Talking Heads, and the dozens of bands that formed in direct response to watching those bands. Concluding that participation was possible. Scene identity formed through repetition rather than scale. You didn't need to play Chicago. You need to play Tuesday.

In London, the 100 Club on Oxford Street became the equivalent node. The 1976 Punk Festival was two nights in September, the Sex Pistols, the Clash, Siouxsie and the Banshees, the Damned sharing bills in a room that held 500 people. It was organized not through national promoters or label infrastructure but through the same hand-to-hand, photocopied-flyer, word-of-mouth network the New York scene had been running for two years. Shows were booked fast. Promotion moved person to person. The economy was immediate and local. Cover charges, not ticket sales, not Ticketmaster, not venue contracts negotiated eighteen months in advance.

The rooms were different. The cities were different. The sounds were different. The structural logic was identical. Build what the circuit won't build in the spaces the circuit doesn't want for the audience the circuit has forgotten exists.

The structural logic of the scene inverts the structural logic of the circuit at every level at once. Small venues eliminate dependence on corporate routing because a room that holds 300 people can be filled through neighborhood reputation rather than national marketing spend. DIY flyers bypass the centralized marketing infrastructure entirely. The music reaches its audience without passing through any filter that might decide it isn't commercial enough to deserve attention. Self-booked shows reduce gatekeeping to its irreducible minimum. If the venue owner will take the door split and you can get enough people in the room, you're on. Repeated local bills strengthen geographic identity. Because repetition builds something a single arena show passing through town can never build. The sense that this music belongs here, that it comes from this specific place and speaks to the people who live in it.

Geography reasserts itself not as nostalgia but as structural necessity. The scene doesn't choose to be local because local is romantic. It chooses to be local because local is the only scale at which the economics work without label investment. Locality is the scene's competitive advantage. The thing the circuit can't replicate because the circuit has optimized away everything that makes a specific place feel specific.

The certainty of this response follows from a simple observation about how power distributes itself. Once circuits centralize authority. Once the decision about who gets to make music at visible scale passes entirely into the hands of label executives, radio programmers, and national promoters — the people excluded from that will build a parallel. Not because they're idealists, though some of them are. Because they need somewhere to play and the existing system won't have them. Touring grids optimize revenue. Scenes optimize participation. When the choice is between a system that might eventually let you in if you spend years qualifying and a system you can build yourself next Tuesday, the second option wins under economic pressure every time.

What the scene restores is that the circuit had eliminated the feedback loop. The direct, immediate, physical relationship between the music being made and the people it's being made for. In a small club, audience and band share the same air. The energy in the room enters the performance in real time. Sets shift from night to night because the band can feel what's working and respond to it without a production manager calculating the cost of the deviation. New bands form weekly because watching a band play badly in a small room is more instructive and more inspiring than watching a band play perfectly from the 40th row of an arena. The barrier between observer and participant is low enough to step over.

That volatility. That sense that anything could happen on any given night had been the first casualty of arena professionalization. The scene brought it back not as an esthetic choice but as a structural condition of operating at a scale where control was neither possible nor desirable.

The counterargument is that local scenes have always existed alongside national circuits. That the club ecosystem predates punk by decades and that punk didn't invent anything structurally new. It simply used infrastructure that was already there. That is accurate as far as it goes. The Marquee in London and the Fillmore in San Francisco and a hundred other rooms had been incubating local music for years before the Sex Pistols played the 100 Club.

But the counterargument misses the reversal. Before punk, local scenes existed in a hierarchical relationship with national circuits. They were at the bottom of a ladder whose top was headlining. The measure of a scene's success was how many of its bands climbed that ladder. Scenes fed circuits. Local intensity was proving ground for national ambition. The circuit was the destination, and the scene was the route.

Punk inverted that relationship completely. The circuit didn't become the enemy — it became irrelevant. National success was optional rather than essential. Local intensity was sufficient rather than preliminary. A band that packed CBGB every Tuesday for six months had accomplished something real and complete, not something that required validation from a label or a national promoter to mean anything. The scene wasn't feeding the circuit. The scene had decided the circuit wasn't worth feeding.

That reversal is the mutation. Not the clubs themselves but the relationship between the clubs and everything above them in the old hierarchy.

If touring grids had loosened and if heavy bands had maintained genuine connections to local club scenes while scaling. If the arena circuit had developed mechanisms for integrating street-level energy rather than processing it out. The frustration that built the scene infrastructure might have diffused before it reached critical mass. Young musicians might have found pathways into the existing system rather than building a parallel one. The gap between street and stage might have remained narrow enough to step across rather than wide enough to require a complete architectural response.

Instead, the gap hardened. Arena looked heavily at the street and saw an audience. Punk looked at the arena and saw a problem. The rooms where distance disappeared weren't built in contrast to the circuit out of romantic preference for small spaces. They were built because the circuit had made itself unreachable. And unreachable things stop being relevant to the people who can't reach them.

Scene over circuit wasn't nostalgic for a simpler time. It was structural correction. The precise and necessary response to a system that had optimized itself into irrelevance for the generation it had originally claimed to represent. When geography was flattened by national routing, punk redrew the map block by block, street by street, room by room. Not with a grand plan. With a photocopied flyer and a Tuesday night booking.

Once local infrastructure proves viable and once it becomes clear that you can build something real and sustaining without the circuit's permission. The fragmentation accelerates. Other cities watch what New York and London built and conclude that the model is portable. The scenes multiply. The map fractures further. And circuits, optimized for consolidation, have no mechanism for responding to a system that has decided consolidation is the problem.

Which sets up everything that follows — scenes multiplying faster than any circuit can contain them, each one generating its own identity, its own bands, its own audience, its own internal pressures toward the next mutation.

IDEOLOGY OVER ATMOSPHERE (1976–1978)

The fog came first. Then someone turned on the lights.

Heavy music in the early 1970's built atmosphere with a slowness that made the darkness feel inevitable rather than constructed. Black Sabbath encoded war, paranoia, and apocalypse in slow looming structures that gave dread a physical dimension. The darkness they summoned felt cosmic precisely because it arrived at such deliberate pace. The riff descending, the tempo refusing to accelerate, the resolution withheld until the tension had accumulated enough weight to mean something. Even when the subject matter was explicitly grounded in the real world. Vietnam in "War Pigs," nuclear anxiety in "Electric Funeral" — the delivery wrapped it in scale and distance. The horror was real, but it arrived through fog. You felt it before you understood it. That mediation was intentional and it was powerful. It gave the music a mythic register that made it feel larger than the specific grievances it described. It was speaking about a condition of existence rather than a list of complaints.

By 1975, that atmosphere had hardened from a living thing into a managed esthetic. Arena lighting rigs reproduced the fog on cue. Leather uniforms codified the visual language of darkness into a reproducible brand. Extended instrumental passages filled the space that atmosphere required without necessarily generating the genuine tension that had made early Sabbath's silences feel dangerous. The myth of heaviness was dark, powerful, larger-than-life. It had stabilized into a set of reliable signals that the audience recognized, and the industry had learned to manufacture on a production schedule. You didn't argue with the system. You invoked demons above it. And the demons showed up on time because they were in the contract.

Into this managed mythology walked 1976 — and 1976 had no patience for myth.

In Britain, the IMF intervention was not an abstraction. It was the government of a developed nation admitting publicly that it could no longer manage its own finances without outside assistance. A humiliation that landed in working-class communities as confirmation of what they had already known for two years. The money was gone. The jobs were gone. The postwar settlement that had promised stability in exchange for labor was revealed as a promise that one side had stopped keeping without bothering to announce it. Youth unemployment climbed. Inflation ate what wages remained. The infrastructure of daily life in cities like London and Manchester and Birmingham was visibly deteriorating. Not declining gracefully but fraying in ways that made the gap between official narrative and lived reality impossible to ignore.

In New York the conditions were different in detail and identical in structure. A city that had once represented the aspirational center of American urban life was functionally bankrupt, its services collapsing, its neighborhoods emptying, its streets carrying a level of visible decay that made cosmic mythology feel not just inadequate but actively insulting. When the rent is due and the job is gone and the city around you is burning sometimes literally, as the South Bronx was demonstrating nightly. Occult abstraction doesn't just feel distant. It feels like a lie told by people who have never had to worry about the rent.

Mythic atmosphere requires a listener with enough stability to suspend immediate reality and enter the myth. By 1976, that suspension was a luxury the audience could no longer afford.

Mutation answered with confrontation -direct, immediate, and deliberately stripped of every mediation that atmosphere had used to maintain its distance from the specific.

The Sex Pistols didn't cloak anger in allegory. "Anarchy in the U.K." — released November 1976 — names the rupture without metaphor, without cosmic framing, without the slow atmospheric buildup that would have given the listener time to process it as something other than a direct address. The monarchy is named. The media is named. The authority structures that had failed the generation singing along are named and antagonized directly. There is no fog. There is no distance. There is no demon invoked above the system. There is just the system, named, and the voice refusing to pretend it deserves respect.

The Ramones operated on different esthetic terrain but the same structural logic. Where the Pistols confronted directly, the Ramones compressed by stripping lyrics down to repetition, urban boredom, and the flat effect of people describing their actual lives without embellishment or mythology. "I Wanna Be Sedated." "Teenage Lobotomy." "Now I Wanna Sniff Some Glue." No fantasy. No darkness summoned from beyond. Just the texture of existence in Forest Hills, Queens, rendered in two minutes and three chords with enough speed to make the compression feel like pressure rather than poverty.

The structural traits that produced this shift follow the ideology with the same precision that punk's musical choices followed its economic conditions. Short songs eliminate the atmospheric buildup that mythic dread requires. You cannot build a fog in ninety seconds, which means you cannot hide behind one. Direct lyrics remove the symbolic distance that allowed arena metal to address real horror while maintaining the aesthetic safety of metaphor. Minimal stage effects strip the mystique that had turned heavy music's darkness into a theatrical experience. No fog machines, no lighting rigs, no production design converting dread into spectacle. Fast attack replaces the looming accumulation of tension with immediate impact. The feeling arrives before the listener has time to process it as art rather than experience.

This is not tonal darkness expanding into unfamiliar territory. It is myth being rejected as a delivery mechanism. The recognition that the distance between the horror and the listener that atmosphere had always maintained was no longer a feature but a failure.

The inevitability follows from the specific nature of the pressure. Atmosphere requires suspension. It requires a listener willing to set aside immediate reality and enter the constructed world the music offers. That willingness is a function of stability. When daily life is sufficiently manageable, the invitation to inhabit a mythic darkness is compelling because it offers something daily life doesn't. When daily life is sufficiently dark. When the rent is genuinely unpayable, the job is genuinely gone, and the city is genuinely deteriorating around you. The invitation to enter a constructed darkness starts to feel like an insult. You don't need the myth. You're living the reality. What you need is someone to acknowledge reality directly, without the fog, without the distance, without the aesthetic mediation that turns genuine horror into a listening experience.

Confrontation requires presence. Presence requires the elimination of distance. And distance — physical, sonic, symbolic, economic — was what arena heavy metal had been building more of with every production upgrade, every ticket price increase, every lighting rig that turned the band into silhouettes against a manufactured darkness.

Punk refuses greatness not because greatness is inherently dishonest but because greatness has become the arena system's primary product. A managed, scheduled, ticketed experience of darkness that required no genuine engagement with the conditions producing it. Punk refuses mysticism for the same reason. It refuses the idea that darkness must be epic to be real, that dread must be cosmic to be legitimate, that the horror of daily life in a deteriorating city requires mythological amplification to deserve musical expression. Instead of summoning apocalypse from beyond the system, punk points at the street and says the apocalypse is already here and has been for some time. Everyone pretending otherwise is either lying or insulated enough from it that their opinion doesn't matter.

The counterargument has genuine historical weight. Heavy metal also addressed politics. "War Pigs" predates punk by six years. "Electric Funeral" addressed nuclear anxiety with a directness that the song's atmospheric delivery sometimes obscures. Confrontation was embedded in metal's DNA from the beginning. The argument that punk introduced political directness to heavy music ignores what heavy music had been making since 1970.

True. And it matters. But the counterargument proves too much, because the distinction being drawn here is not about subject matter. It is about delivery. It's about the distance between the darkness and the listener, about whether the confrontation is mediated through atmosphere or delivered without it.

Sabbath's confrontation arrived through fog. The slow build, the ominous tone, the metaphorical framing. All of it created a buffer between the horror being described and the listener receiving it. That buffer was part of the power. It gave the darkness a mythic scale that made it feel like a condition of existence rather than a specific grievance. But it also gave the listener somewhere to stand, which wasn't inside the thing being described. You could feel the weight of "War Pigs" without having to confront the specific, immediate, personal reality at which it was pointing. The atmosphere provided aesthetic distance that was at once the source of the music's power and the mechanism of its detachment.

Punk collapsed the buffer. It accelerates the tempo so there is no time for atmospheric growth. It removes the sonic space that dread requires to build. It shortens the argument to the point where the only thing left is the point. No buildup. No grandeur. No mythic register that elevates the specific grievance into something larger than itself. Just the grievance, named, at speed, in a room small enough that the person naming it is standing close enough to touch.

The difference is not subject matter. It is scale of address. Metal speaks about collapse from a position of mythic distance. Punk speaks directly at the system from inside the collapse. One is a diagnosis delivered from outside the condition. The other is a scream from inside it.

If heavy music had stripped back its own myth in the mid-

1970's. If it had returned to smaller venues, reduced the spectacle, sharpened the lyrical directness that had always been present underneath the atmospheric delivery — the rupture might have looked entirely different. A heavy music that acknowledged its own theatrical excess and corrected for it voluntarily might have absorbed the confrontational energy that punk was generating rather than producing it as an opposing force. The directness, the rawness, the refusal of distance. These were not foreign to heavy music's original instincts. They were present in early Sabbath before the production budgets arrived and the lighting rigs went up. A conscious return to those instincts might have made the rupture unnecessary.

Instead, heavy music doubled down. The spectacle increased. The myth solidified. The aesthetic codification that had begun as a practical response to arena scale became an identity so thoroughly established that any deviation from it read as failure rather than evolution. The leather stayed. The fog remained. The extended passages stayed. The distance between the darkness in the music and the darkness in the street grew wider with every album cycle, every tour, every production upgrade that made the experience more impressive and less honest.

So, punk rejected not heaviness itself but the myth that had grown around it. The theatrical apparatus that had converted genuine dread into a scheduled experience, genuine darkness into a brand, genuine confrontation into a performance of confrontation. All delivered from behind a barricade to an audience in numbered seats. The rejection was surgical. It removed the theater and left the dread intact. The speed, the aggression, the refusal of resolution. These are heavy. The three-chord vocabulary, the two-minute song, the confrontational delivery. These are the bones of heaviness stripped of everything the industry has added to make heaviness more manageable and more profitable.

Confrontation over atmosphere. Ideology over aura. The darkness doesn't need a fog machine. It's already in the room.

When darkness becomes theatrical the next mutation removes the theater. Not because theater is inherently dishonest but because theater has become the mechanism. The industry maintained the distance between the music and the people it was supposed to speak for. Remove the theater and the distance collapses. Remove the distance and the music is dangerous again. Not dangerous as a brand attribute. Dangerous as a living condition.

Under pressure, youth don't want myth. They want impact. They want the darkness acknowledged without mediation, the anger expressed without aesthetic elevation, the reality of their lives reflected at them without the fog that makes it look epic rather than immediate. Punk provided that. And in providing it, it didn't destroy heavy music's legacy. It stripped it back to its foundation and asked what load was bearing.

The answer, as the following years would demonstrate, was more than anyone expected.

PUNK'S INTERNAL INSTABILITY (1977–1979)

Punk solved access. It restores geography. It replaced myth with confrontation. It built infrastructure from the ground up into rooms that the arena circuit had never bothered to want.

And then it ran directly into the problem that every successful rupture eventually faces. The problem of what comes after the walls come down.

Every mutation carries its own instability inside it from the beginning. The traits that make a rupture explosive are precisely the traits that make it unsustainable at scale. Speed creates momentum but not durability. Immediacy generates energy but not architecture. The rejection of structure is a powerful force for demolition and a poor foundation for construction. Punk had been built to break things, and it was extraordinarily good at that. But breaking things is different from building something that can survive the morning after the demolition.

By 1977, success arrived faster than infrastructure could handle. Not commercial success in the arena sense. Punk hadn't built toward that and didn't want it. But the specific and dangerous success of becoming a cultural phenomenon large enough to attract the attention of the systems it had defined itself against. The media noticed. The labels noticed. The tabloids noticed. And the attention that punk had used as a weapon — the confrontation, the provocation, the deliberate antagonism toward every institution with a stake in maintaining order. This turned out to be a weapon that cut in both directions.

The Sex Pistols detonated British media cycles with a precision that Malcolm McLaren had engineered deliberately. The Bill Grundy interview in December 1976. The tabloid front pages. The banned tours. The questions in Parliament. Each confrontation was designed to make the establishment look ridiculous and the Pistols look dangerous. For a period of months, it worked exactly as intended. But the media cycle that punk had weaponized ran on acceleration. Each confrontation had to be more extreme than the last to maintain the same level of attention, and acceleration without structure has only one destination. Within a year of "Anarchy in the U.K." charting, the Sex Pistols had imploded. The very exposure punk used as confrontation had destabilized it from the inside. The band's internal contradictions amplified by the spotlight until they became impossible to contain.

That is the first instability. Acceleration without structure. A movement that had built its identity on going faster had no mechanism for deciding when to stop.

The second instability operated at the infrastructure level. Punk scenes had been built around the specific conditions of small rooms. The 300-capacity venue, the self-organized bill, the DIY network that ran on personal relationships and photocopied flyers. Those conditions were not just practical constraints. They were the source of the music's energy. The proximity, the volatility, the sense that anything could happen. All of it depended on operating at a scale where control was neither possible nor necessary.

When the crowds multiplied, the conditions that had

generated the energy began to dissolve. CBGB had been designed for a scene. It had not been designed for a movement. When the movement arrived — when the word spread beyond the neighborhood, beyond the city, beyond the original participants who had built the thing from nothing. The rooms strained under the weight of their own success. Violence increased as the audience expanded beyond the community that had established the scene's informal codes. Police presence followed violence. The intimacy that had made the experience feel genuinely dangerous got replaced by a different kind of danger that had nothing to do with music and everything to do with crowd management. The DIY networks that had functioned elegantly at 200 people buckled at 2,000 because DIY networks are built on trust and shared understanding and those things don't scale automatically with ticket sales.

Access scales poorly. That is not a failure of punk's vision — it is a structural reality that the vision had no mechanism for addressing because addressing it would have required building exactly the kind of infrastructure that punk had defined itself against.

The third instability was ideological and, in some ways, the most corrosive because it operated from inside the movement's own logic. Punk had replaced heavy metal's unifying myth with confrontation. But confrontation, unlike myth, has no stabilizing center. Myth provides a shared narrative that holds a community together even when its members disagree about specifics. Confrontation provides energy and direction but no common ground beyond the thing being confronted. Once the targets began to fragment — once different factions identified different enemies and different solutions — the confrontational energy that had unified the rupture turned inward with the same force it had previously directed outward.

The Clash made the ideological contradiction visible in a way that no other band in the movement could match. Formed in London in 1976 from the same scene infrastructure that had produced the Sex Pistols, the Clash began as a three-chord punk band with explicit political commitments and a sound that could have been made with the gear available at any pawnshop in Notting Hill. By London Calling in 1979 they were recording a double album that moved through reggae, rockabilly, jazz, and funk with an ambition and musical sophistication that the original punk template had defined itself against. By the early 1980s they were filling arenas. The band that had rejected the arena system had become the arena system. Not through betrayal of their principles but through the logical consequence of those principles applied to the reality of sustaining a band on a scale over time.

The Clash didn't fail punk. They demonstrated punk's structural problem with more clarity than any collapse could have managed. You can start in the small room. You can maintain political commitment. You can keep the confrontational energy directed outward rather than inward. And you will still end up in the arena if you survive long enough and reach enough people, because the arena is where the circuit takes everything that works. The only way to avoid the arena is to not work — and the Clash worked extraordinarily well.

Others pushed political messaging further left, explicitly aligning punk's anger with socialist politics and third-world solidarity. Others leaned into pure nihilism. The rejection of meaning itself as the only honest response to a world that had demonstrated its own meaninglessness. Some prioritized fashion and shock, treating punk as an aesthetic project rather than a political one. The disagreements were genuine and irreconcilable because they were disagreements about what punk was. Whether the confrontation was a means to an end or an end in itself, about whether the goal was to build something or simply to destroy what existed.

Without a unifying myth — and punk had rejected myth deliberately and correctly for reasons that remained valid — there was no stabilizing narrative to hold these factions together once the initial energy of the rupture began to dissipate. The confrontation turned inward. Scenes fractured. The energy that had been directed at the arena system began to be directed at other punks who weren't doing it right, weren't political enough, weren't nihilistic enough, weren't authentic enough by whatever definition of authenticity the faction had adopted.

The structural traits that had made punk explosive amplified the fracture rather than containing it. Short songs provided limited room for structural evolution. Once the two-minute three-chord template was established, the only directions available were faster, slower, more political, less political, louder, quieter. The minimal harmonic vocabulary reached saturation quickly because there are only so many ways to arrange three chords before the combinations begin to feel exhausted. Fast production cycles meant records arrived before ideas had fully developed. The anti-virtuosity stance established a technical ceiling that some musicians found liberating and others found suffocating. The ones who found it suffocating began looking for ways over it.

The very traits that had made punk explosive had a half-life. The explosion was real. The aftermath was inevitable.

The deepest instability was philosophical, and it was built into punk's foundation from the first note. Punk defined itself through negation. It existed to oppose arena polish, label hierarchy, mythic distance, technical gatekeeping, corporate routing, and the managed darkness that heavy music had become. That negation was the source of its power and its clarity. When you know exactly what you're against, the argument is simple and the energy is focused. The communities join around the shared target with a speed that more constructive movements rarely achieve.

But negation has a structural problem that becomes visible the moment it succeeds. Once the targets have been named and the walls have been torn down — once the arena system has been demonstrated to be irrelevant, the technical hierarchy has been rejected, and the myth has been stripped of its theatrical apparatus — the question that negation cannot answer emerges with full force. What next? What does the movement build in the space where the thing it destroyed used to stand? What does confrontation look like when there is nothing left to confront, or when the things left to confront are internal rather than external?

Opposition cannot sustain itself forever without transformation. The energy that negation generates is real, but it is not renewable on its own terms. At some point the movement must decide what it is for rather than only what it is against. That decision is the moment when the unified rupture becomes a collection of diverging responses to the same original pressure.

The counterargument is that punk did evolve. That post-punk, hardcore, and new wave represent not a collapse but a diversification, and that instability was the mechanism of that diversification rather than evidence of failure. That is correct. And it proves the mutation thesis precisely.

By 1978 and 1979, the original three-chord minimalism was fragmenting along every fault line simultaneously. In New York, bands that had formed in the CBGB crucible began pushing into art-damaged experimentation. Television's intricate guitar architecture that treated the instrument as a system of interlocking melodic voices rather than a rhythm tool. Talking Heads' angular funk-influenced structures that absorbed African rhythmic ideas into a rock framework without softening either. The no-wave scene pushed further still — deliberately embracing atonality, noise, and structural chaos as confrontational tools, treating it as an ideological position. The minimalism that had been punk's entry point became a launching pad for musicians who had used access to get into the room and then discovered they had more to say than three chords could contain.

In the UK, the response moved in the opposite direction.

Where New York pushed toward complexity, London pushed toward intensification. Joy Division — formed in Manchester in 1976 in direct response to seeing the Sex Pistols play — took punk's confrontational energy and stripped it further, building a sound of such deliberate bleakness that it made early Sabbath's atmosphere seem almost hopeful by comparison. The aggression of the original punk template was replaced by a controlled, suffocating despair that had no interest in the three-chord energy of the Pistols. It carried punk's rejection of comfort and transcendence into territory the original movement hadn't mapped. Wire, formed in London in 1976, took a different approach — reducing rock music to its structural elements with an intellectual rigor that treated each song as a problem to be solved in the minimum number of moves, producing records of such concentrated economy that they made the Ramones sound sprawling.

Hardcore scenes formed in direct response to two simultaneous threats. Commercial co-option, as major labels began signing punk acts and smoothing their edges for radio, and internal drift, as the original movement's ideological coherence dissolved into competing factions. Hardcore was punk's answer to punk's own betrayal of punk. A recursion that demonstrated both the movement's strength and its instability.

The system destabilized because pure access without development reaches balance quickly. Access solves the entry problem. It does not solve the question of what you do once you are inside. Once anyone can start a band, the question of what distinguishes one band from another reasserts itself.

Not as a gatekeeping mechanism but as a genuine artistic question that the three-chord vocabulary could not answer indefinitely.

If punk had institutionalized — had built stable mid-sized venues, sustainable touring circuits, moderate technical standards that allowed development without demanding virtuosity. It might have remained a unified movement longer. The energy might have been sustained. The community might have held together. The fragmentation might have been delayed.

But institutionalization would have required building exactly the infrastructure that punk had defined itself against. Stable venues require booking systems. Sustainable touring requires routing. Moderate technical standards require someone to decide what the standards are. Every one of those requirements is a step back toward the hierarchy that the rupture had been designed to demolish. Punk could not institutionalize without ceasing to be punk. The fragmentation wasn't a failure of nerves or a betrayal of principles. It was the logical consequence of principles that were incompatible with institutional survival.

So, the movement fragmented. And the fragmentation was the most generative thing it could have done.

The fragmentation created pressure in multiple directions at once. The directions it created were not random. They followed the same structural logic that had produced punk in the first place. Which is to say they followed the specific shape of the dissatisfactions that punk's own limitations had generated.

Some bands reintroduced complexity. Not the arena metal complexity of extended solos and dual-guitar harmonies engineered for spectacle. But a new kind of complexity that had absorbed punk's confrontational directness. It was now asking what happened when you applied that directness to more sophisticated structures. Post-punk didn't abandon punk's rejection of myth. It asked what came after the rejection. The complexity returned but it returned through punk's door rather than through the arenas.

Some bands increased speed and aggression beyond what the original punk template had imagined possible. Hardcore took the three-chord vocabulary and the confrontational delivery and pushed both past their natural limits — faster, shorter, louder, more politically uncompromising, more deliberately inaccessible to anyone outside the community that had built it. Where punk had rejected the arena system's gatekeeping, hardcore rejected the gatekeeping that punk itself had begun to develop as it achieved visibility. The rupture ruptured. The correction corrected itself.

Some bands began pulling the heaviness back in. The riff, the weight, the sonic density that punk had stripped away as part of its rejection of arena metal's mythology. The early crossover acts recognized that what punk had rejected wasn't heaviness itself but the institutional apparatus surrounding it. Strip the apparatus and the heaviness remained available. The weight of a Sabbath riff didn't require a lighting rig or a leather uniform or a 20,000-seat arena to mean something. It just required the willingness to use it without asking permission. Which punk had already established was everyone's right.

The system began recombining. The walls that punk had torn down didn't stay down as empty space. They became raw material. The bricks got used to build something new that carried punk's structural corrections inside it while reaching back toward the heaviness that punk had temporarily set aside in the urgency of the demolition.

Punk was necessary. Without the rupture, the arena system's consolidation would have continued unchallenged. The technical hierarchy would have risen further. The geographic homogenization would have deepened. The managed darkness would have become the only darkness available. Punk broke the scale, restored access, and returned the music to the street and those are permanent contributions to the architecture of heavy music regardless of how briefly the original movement held together as a unified force.

But punk's internal volatility was never a design flaw. It was a design feature that the designers hadn't fully anticipated. Once you remove permission you also remove guardrails. Once you establish that anyone can make music on their own terms you cannot then specify what those terms must be. Once the ladder is torn down, the space it occupies doesn't stay empty. It fills with whatever the people who tore it down decide to build, and those people have different ideas, different influences, different dissatisfactions, and different visions of what the music should become.

Without any guardrails, the mutation accelerates. The recombination that began in 1978 and 1979 would produce, within the following decade, a proliferation of heavy forms that the original mutation could not have predicted and the arena system could not have contained. Forms that carried punk's structural lessons inside them while recovering the weight and the darkness and the mythic register that punk had temporarily suspended in the urgency of tearing down the walls.

Chapter 4 examined the rupture from four angles — access, geography, ideology, instability — because the rupture itself operated on all four levels simultaneously. Punk did not succeed because it had better music or more authentic anger or a superior political vision. It succeeded because the system it ruptured had created the precise conditions that made rupture inevitable, and punk was the form that the inevitability took.

The instability that closes this chapter is not a failure of the argument. It is the argument. Every mutation in the history of heavy music has carried its own correction inside it — the seed of the next rupture embedded in the structure of the current one. Heavy music scaled and produced the conditions for punk. Punk ruptured and produced the conditions for what followed. The system does not reach equilibrium. It produces pressure, pressure produces mutation, mutation produces new pressure, and the cycle continues with energy that three chords and a two-minute song released back into the world in 1976 and that has not been fully contained since.

Chapter 5 will examine the recombination — the specific forms that emerged when punk's structural corrections met the heaviness that had never gone away, and what happened when a generation that had learned it didn't need permission decided to pick up the weight again.

CHAPTER FIVE

when Speed Became Identity

SPEED AS ESCALATION (1978–1982)

Punk stripped the system down. Hardcore compresses it until the structure nearly breaks.

The professionalization that punk had ruptured was gone. The technical hierarchy had been dismantled. The arena circuit had been declared irrelevant. The three-chord vocabulary, the two-minute song, the small room, the photocopied flyer — these had become the operating conditions of a generation that had decided it didn't need permission. By 1978, those conditions had normalized. And normalization is the beginning of the next problem.

Compression stabilizes quickly. Once every band plays fast, loud, and short and once the template that had felt revolutionary in 1976 has been adopted by hundreds of bands in dozens of cities. The intensity plateaus. The energy that had made punk feel genuinely dangerous becomes predictable. Predictability is the thing punk had defined itself against. And a movement defined by the rejection of predictability cannot tolerate becoming predictable without producing a correction.

At the same time, the external pressure that had generated punk was not easing. It was sharpening.

Reagan's election in 1980 landed in American urban communities as something more than a political shift. It was the announcement of a governing philosophy that had no interest in the economic conditions of the cities that had produced punk and hardcore. Thatcher's parallel project in the UK had been running since 1979, dismantling the social infrastructure that working-class communities had depended on with an ideological conviction that made the IMF crisis of 1976 look like a temporary setback. Urban decay deepened. Youth unemployment climbed. Police presence at shows increased as hardcore scenes became visible enough to attract institutional attention. Violence around scenes rose not as chaos but as the logical physical expression of an anger that had no other available outlet.

The tension was structural and it was precise. Punk's template — built specifically to match the pressure of 1976 — no longer matched the pressure of 1980. The pressure had increased. The template did not. Something had to give.

Mutation escalates through speed. Not as an aesthetic preference but as the only available lever when everything else has already been stripped away.

In Los Angeles, Black Flag pushed tempos beyond anything the late-1970's punk template had established as a ceiling. Songs collapsed toward a minute, then under it. Riffs became percussive bludgeons not melodic statements to be followed but rhythmic impacts to be absorbed. The space that even the Ramones had maintained between sections disappeared entirely. Henry Rollins' arrival as vocalist in 1981 added physical intensity to the delivery that matched the musical compression. A presence that made the confrontation feel bodily rather than merely sonic. A Black Flag show in a 200-capacity room in Los Angeles in 1981 was not a performance in any arena sense of the word. It was an environment of controlled aggression that the audience entered and either survived or died.

In Washington D.C., Minor Threat tightened songs into bursts that made the Ramones' two-minute format seem leisurely. Songs ran ninety seconds. Sixty seconds. Sometimes less. The attack was immediate — no introduction, no ramp-up, no moment of orientation before the full force of the thing arrived. The songs didn't build to anything. They were already at maximum intensity when they began, and they ended before the audience had fully processed what had happened. Ian MacKaye's delivery carried a moral urgency that the anarchic wing of punk had specifically rejected. Not anger without direction but anger with a precise target. A precise argument about what the target deserved.

In San Francisco, the Dead Kennedys injected their manic tempo shifts and rhythmic instability that added a different dimension to the escalation. Where Black Flag compressed through consistency and Minor Threat through brevity, the Dead Kennedys used unpredictability as an additional source of pressure. The tempo lurching, the attack shifting, the satirical content of Jello Biafra's lyrics operating in deliberate contrast to the sonic violence surrounding it. The humor was still present, but it had been weaponized. It landed harder because it arrived inside something that made comfort impossible.

These three scenes — Los Angeles, Washington D.C., San Francisco were developing at the same time and independently. Connected by tape trading networks and touring circuits that the bands themselves were building rather than inheriting. The infrastructure was DIY by necessity and by ideology simultaneously. You didn't wait for a booking agent. You called the venue, booked the show, loaded the van, drove through the night, played to whoever showed up, and drove to the next city. Black Flag's touring schedule in the early 1980s was an exercise in logistical endurance that most arena acts would have found unconceivable. Not because the resources weren't available but because the infrastructure of the arena circuit had no mechanism for what Black Flag was doing. They were operating in the spaces the circuit didn't want.

The structural consequences of speed escalation follow with the same logic that had governed every previous mutation. Tempo doubling relative to the 1977 punk baseline meant that rhythmic information arriving at the listener doubled as well. The brain processes twice as many beats per minute, the body responding with a physical urgency that slower music couldn't generate. Songs shrinking further meant that energy density per second increased even as total duration decreased. Drumming shifted toward relentless high-BPM propulsion that required a specific and demanding precision. Not the precision of the arena metal drummer executing a choreographed fill on cue, but the precision of an engine running at red line without seizing. The downstroke patterns that punk had established accelerated into near-continuous assault that left no space for breath, for recovery, for the moment of release that conventional song structure provides.

Energy density increases. Atmosphere disappears entirely.

There is no slow dread in hardcore. No theatrical pause. No

mythic framing. Not even punk's loose swagger remains. It has tightened into sprint, into the forward lean of something running at full speed with no intention of stopping. The comparison to early Sabbath is not an accident. Both represent the logical endpoint of a specific kind of pressure applied to a specific musical form. Sabbath took the blues and removed its resolution. Hardcore took punk and removed its breath.

This is not simplification. The counterargument that hardcore represents a failure of ambition — that bands played fast and short because they lacked the skill to do anything more complex — needs to be addressed directly and defeated completely. Speed requires precision. Sustaining 200 beats per minute across a set without collapse demands a tightness that is qualitatively different from but not less than the tightness required to execute a dual-guitar harmony at arena volume. Black Flag rehearsed obsessively. Minor Threat's rhythmic precision was a conscious achievement rather than a happy accident. The Dead Kennedys' tempo shifts required the kind of locked band communication that only comes from playing together constantly and listening to each other with full attention. The aggression was controlled. The reduction of atmosphere was deliberate. Dead space was weakness in a context where weakness meant losing the audience's physical engagement. And physical engagement was the only currency the scene ran on.

Escalation was inevitable because once access is normalized the three-chord vocabulary and the two-minute song have become the common language of a generation. The only available lever for variation and increased impact is compression. You cannot remove more chords. You cannot shorten songs indefinitely. But you can increase the speed at which the existing elements arrive. Speed changes the physical experience of music in ways that no other variable can replicate. Hardcore treats time as the enemy. Not time in the cosmic sense that heavy metal had addressed, but time in the immediate sense of the seconds between the beginning of a song and its maximum impact. Every second buildup is a second of distance. Hardcore eliminates the distance.

The audience response shifted to match the musical escalation. Moshing became more physically violent. Not as an expression of chaos but as the appropriate kinetic response to music that made stillness feel physiologically impossible. Stage diving accelerated. The pit became a space of ritualized physical release. it served the same function for the hardcore audience that atmospheric dread had served for the early Sabbath audience. A sanctioned experience of something that daily life both generated and suppressed. The show was no longer a communal gathering. It was a kinetic confrontation with everything outside the room.

If punk had expanded harmonically in the late 1970s — had embraced mid-tempo groove, had moved toward the art-rock hybrids the New York scene was beginning to develop — hardcore might never have formed as a distinct mutation. The escalation might have been absorbed into a broader musical evolution that increased complexity without increasing aggression. Youth frustration might have found its expression in sophistication rather than compression.

But external pressure doesn't ease because the music

decides to get more sophisticated. Reagan and Thatcher were not responding to the aesthetic choices of punk musicians. The policing of shows was not calibrated to the harmonic vocabulary of the bands being policed. The economic conditions that had generated anger did not improve because the music that expressed the anger found a more nuanced form. Under rising tension, music doesn't soften. It compresses. Hardcore was not a choice. It was a measurement of the external pressure taken in musical units.

Hardcore doesn't abandon punk's principles. It turns into the dial until the structure nearly breaks. Once tempo reaches its structural limits — once the human body can no longer play faster without the music ceasing to be music and becoming noise. A new question emerges with full force.

What happens when speed alone isn't enough?

MILITANCY OVER AMBIGUITY (1979–1982)

Punk tolerated ambiguity. Hardcore burns it out.

The looseness that had been one of punk's real strengths — the spacious tent that contained art-school experimentation in New York and political agitation in London, nihilism and fashion and humor and real working-class rage — was also what made punk hard to keep up as a coherent movement under growing external pressure. Ambiguity prevails if there is enough stability to support multiple positions at once. As the environment tightens, ambiguity begins to present itself as a lack of conviction. And with no conviction, in a movement characterized by confrontation, can begin to appear as weakness. By 1979, the environment had hardened considerably. Reagan's America and Thatcher's Britain were not abstract political conditions. They were the everyday reality for young people living in cities that their states understood they were clearly deprioritized. Their governing philosophies had concluded that the social contract was a luxury that the economy can't afford anymore. The recession deepened. Urban violence rose. The police showed up at hardcore shows not because the shows were violent. But because visible youth subcultures won institutional attention with little interest in distinguishing between the music and the threat it posed. The media satirized hardcore: it is chaos, its dangers, the visible result of a social breakdown that the governing ideology was at once causing and attributing blame to. The stakes are also that, and doubt begins to seem brittle. Hardcore rebuts with militancy. Not as a foreign ideology but as the emergent product of a movement that had no sense of who it was or what it was defending. In Washington D.C., Minor Threat articulated straight edge and in doing so changed the structural logic of scene participation in ways that are still working themselves out forty years later. The straight edge codes — no drinking, no drugs, no self-destruction. Not presented as rules imposed from outside but as commitments made from inside. A refusal to participate in the self-destruction that the system was offering as the primary available comfort to the generation it had failed. MacKaye's logic was structural rather than moralistic. The system wants you drunk and compliant. Sobriety is a form of resistance. Clarity is a weapon. The X marked on the hand was borrowed from the practice of marking underage attendees at shows. It became the most legible symbol of a movement that had decided readability was strength rather than compromise.

The significance of straight edge extends beyond its specific behavioral codes. It represents the first moment in hardcore's history when belonging became conditional. When participation in the scene required not just showing up and paying the cover charge but demonstrating alignment with a set of values the scene had decided were non-negotiable. Access remained low in economic terms. Cheap gear. Small rooms. DIY networks. Anyone could still start a band and book a show. But belonging to a genuine membership in the community rather than mere physical presence at its events had acquired criteria. That is a structural shift as significant as any musical one.

In Los Angeles, Black Flag cultivated a different but related form of militancy. Where Minor Threat's hardening was ideological Black Flag's was physical and relentless. The touring schedule Greg Ginn maintained was not a commercial operation. It was a demonstration of endurance as ideology. The band playing every city, every room, every night, not because the economics justified it but because stopping would have been a form of the comfort they were rejecting. The confrontational shows, the us-versus-them posture the band cultivated deliberately, the physical intensity of the performances. These were not marketing. They were the content. The message was the endurance itself. That you could keep going under conditions that the mainstream had decided made going impossible.

The visual codes of hardcore hardened in parallel with the ideological ones. Short hair replaced the mohawks and colored spikes of the earlier punk aesthetic. Not as a fashion choice but as a deliberate rejection of fashion, a refusal to let the music's identity be defined by an image the mainstream could appropriate and sell. Boots. Stripped-down clothing. The visual vocabulary of work rather than performance. The hardcore look said: this is not a costume. The arena metal look said: this is exactly a costume. The distinction was intentional and structural. An argument made through appearance around what the music was for and to whom it belonged.

Show etiquette hardened alongside the visual codes. The pit became a proving ground — not for violence in a random sense but for the specific physical courage required to enter a space of controlled collision and remain standing. Moshing shifted from the chaotic dancing of the early punk shows to something more ritualized. A collision ritual with its own protocols, its own codes of conduct, its own hierarchy of respect that had nothing to do with technical musicianship and everything to do with physical commitment. You proved you're belonging not by playing well or knowing the right people but by entering the pit and absorbing what it offered without flinching. Physical endurance became the currency of membership in a community that had decided endurance was the appropriate response to the external conditions it was operating.

The hardening follows directly from the pressure that produced it. Once a scene defines itself through opposition to a specific set of conditions — and the conditions are Reagan's America and Thatcher's Britain and the policing and the recession and the urban decay. It must develop internal coherence as a survival strategy. A movement without internal coherence gets diluted. It gets co-opted. It gets absorbed by the mainstream it defined itself against. Its symbols stripped of meaning and sold back to the audience as fashion. Clear codes prevent dilution. Militancy replaces punk's loose irony not because irony was wrong but because irony requires a stable enough environment to register as irony rather than confusion. Under sufficient pressure, the gap between irony and sincerity closes. Hardcore closed it deliberately.

The counterargument is that hardcore was not uniformly militant. That some scenes retained humor and openness, that the characterization of the movement as ideologically rigid ignores the genuine diversity that existed within it. That is true. The Dead Kennedys maintained satirical irony throughout their most intense period. The Boston scene developed its own character distinct from D.C.'s straight edge militancy. Regional variation was real and significant.

But the dominant structural trend favored tightening. The dominant structural trend is what this argument is tracking. Faster tempos left less room for the kind of ironic distance that humor requires. You cannot deliver a punchline at 220 beats per minute in a way that lands as a punchline rather than as another sonic impact. Shorter songs left less room for the kind of contextual setup that makes satire clear. The more intense the sound became; the less structural space remained for aesthetic drift. Militancy scaled with speed because speed and militancy were both responses to the same external pressure. And that pressure was not asking for nuance.

If punk's ambiguity had remained dominant — if the scenes of the early 1980s had tolerated broad stylistic and behavioral variance, had allowed the art-school experimentation of the New York scene to coexist peacefully with the political militancy of D.C. and the physical aggression of Los Angeles. Then hardcore might have evolved as a purely sonic shift without the ideological hardening. The energy could have escalated without the tribal boundaries setting. The music could have gotten faster without belonging or conditional.

But the external conditions didn't allow that evolution. The pressure hardening the music was the same pressure hardening the communities the music came from. When the environment outside the scene offers nothing — no economic stability, no political representation, no cultural validation, no pathway into the mainstream, that doesn't require abandoning everything the scene values. The scene turns inward and builds its identity from what it can control. It controls its codes. It controls its space. It controls who belongs and on what terms. That is not tribalism in the harsh sense. It is the rational response of a community under sustained pressure to the need for internal logic.

Hardcore solved punk's diffusion problem by sharpening its focus. The trade-off was that sharpening cuts both ways. Participation survived — the economic barriers remained low, the DIY infrastructure remained intact, the small rooms remained accessible. But belonging became conditional in ways that generated their own fractures. Straight edge versus non-straight edge. Political versus apolitical. Controlled aggression versus chaos. The internal disputes that had fragmented punk along ideological lines began to fragment hardcore along behavioral ones. Scenes split. Sub-scenes formed. The coherence that militancy had created became the source of the next instability.

And underneath all of it, a question that the speed and the militancy and the behavioral codes had temporarily suppressed was beginning to reassert itself. The music had gotten as fast as it could get. The ideology had gotten as tight as it could get. The identity had gotten as clearly defined as it could get. And the external pressure — the recession, the dismantling, the policing, the urban decay — had not responded to any of it by easing.

What happens when maximum intensity still isn't enough? When the speed and the clarity and physical endurance and the behavioral codes have all been deployed and the thing you're pushing against is still there, still pushing back, still indifferent to the force you're bringing against it?

You look for more weight.

REINFORCEMENT THROUGH WEIGHT (1982–1985)

By 1982, hardcore had reached its structural ceiling and the ceiling was visible from every direction at once.

Tempo was maxed. The human body has bodily limits on how fast it can play a stringed instrument with precision. Hardcore had found those limits. Songs were under a minute.

Identity codes were rigid. Scenes were splitting along behavioral and ideological fault lines that the music's own militancy had created. The DIY infrastructure sustaining the movement was straining under the weight of an audience that had grown faster than the infrastructure could accommodate. The external pressure that had generated the escalation — Reagan, Thatcher, the recession, the policing — had not responded to maximum intensity by retreating. It had responded by continuing to exist.

Speed alone could not carry further escalation. The dial had been turned as far as it would go. Something else was needed.

At the same time, a parallel mutation was developing in a system that hardcore had explicitly rejected but never fully escaped. Traditional heavy metal — arena-codified, leather-uniformed, production-polished — had professionalized to the point of self-parody by the early 1980s. The NWOBHM had injected new energy into British metal at the end of the 1970s, producing bands that carried genuine aggression and technical ambition. But even that energy was processed through the arena system's requirements. The production cleaning up, the image standardizing, the songs enlarging for radio. The distance between the metal mainstream and the street-level reality of the audience it claimed to represent was approaching the same gap that had generated punk in the first place.

Underneath the mainstream, a parallel metal mutation was forming that had absorbed both the NWOBHM's technical ambition and hardcore's structural lessons without fully belonging to either.

In the Bay Area, Metallica were doing something the existing categories could not cleanly contain. The NWOBHM influence was audible. The dual-guitar architecture, the technical precision, the willingness to write songs that developed over multiple minutes rather than collapsing into hardcore brevity. But the production was raw in ways that arena metal had specifically optimized away. The tempos were faster than metal had previously sustained. The riffs carried a percussive aggression that owed as much to hardcore's rhythmic attack as to any British metal precedent. The songs were long, but they didn't feel long. They felt dense, compressed, and driven by an internal logic that had more in common with the urgency of hardcore than with the spectacle of arena metal.

In the UK, Discharge had been operating since the late 1970s at the intersection of punk, hardcore, and metal without acknowledging the intersection as such. Their approach — slightly slower than peak hardcore velocity but saturated with a tonal density and distortion depth that punk's minimal gear aesthetic couldn't generate. It produced something that felt genuinely new without announcing itself as a genre. The D-beat drumming pattern that Discharge established became one of the most imitated rhythmic approaches in the history of heavy music precisely because it solved a specific problem: how to maintain hardcore's urgency at a tempo that allowed the guitar tone to develop enough low-end weight to feel physically crushing rather than merely fast.

Two systems were moving toward each other. The movement was not coordinated. It was structural. The consequence of two forms hitting their respective ceilings simultaneously and discovering that the other form contained the solution to the problem the ceiling represented.

Hardcore's ceiling was speed saturation and ideological fracture. The music had gotten as fast as it could get and the community had gotten as tight as it could get and neither had produced the escalation in impact that the external pressure seemed to demand. What was missing was weight. The low-end physical presence, the tonal density, the riff as blunt instrument rather than rhythmic barrage. Metal had weight. Metal had always had weight. What metal had lost, in its arena arrangement, was the urgency, the rawness, the refusal of distance that hardcore had built its entire identity around.

Metal's ceiling was arena codification and the loss of volatility. The polish the production system had applied to heavy music had cleaned away the qualities that made it feel dangerous. The murk, the uncertainty, the sense that the music was operating at the edge of its own control. What metal needed was not more production. It needed less. It needed the structural compression that hardcore had perfected. It needed shorter songs, rawer production, faster tempos, a rhythmic attack that prioritized impact over spectacle.

Under pressure, adjacent forms merge to regain the escalation capacity that each has lost individually.

The physical spaces where this recombination happened were not arenas and were not 200-capacity hardcore clubs either. They were the mid-sized venues — 500 to 2,000 capacities — in cities like San Francisco, New York, and Los

Angeles, and they were the tape trading networks that moved cassettes of live shows and demos across geographic distances that touring circuits hadn't yet connected. A kid in New Jersey in 1983 could have a tape of a Metallica rehearsal and a tape of a Cro-Mags show and a tape of a Discharge record and could hear the conversation happening between them before any of the participants had necessarily heard each other's music in real time. The recombination spread faster than the touring did because of the infrastructure for it. The tape, the photocopied zine, the network of people already paying attention to both systems had already existed.

In New York, the Cro-Mags made fusion explicit by 1985. Formed from the hardcore scene that CBGB had generated — the same infrastructure, the same DIY booking, the same physical proximity to the audience. The Cro-Mags brought a guitar tone and a riff vocabulary that had no precedent in pure hardcore. The low-end weight was metal. The delivery was hardcore. The songs had the structural compression of the D.C. scene and the tonal density of something that had been listening to Black Sabbath without apologizing for it. The Cro-Mags didn't sound like a compromise between two forms. They sounded like a new form that had absorbed both and exceeded either.

In California, the early thrash scene was executing the same recombination from the metal side. Metallica, Slayer, and Exodus were taking the technical architecture of the NWOBHM and subjecting it to the structural compression and rhythmic aggression of hardcore. Not as a conscious genre exercise but as the natural consequence of musicians who had grown up listening to both and decided that the ceiling of each was best broken by importing the floor of the other. The riffs got heavier. The tempos accelerated. The production stripped back toward rawness. The songs kept the developmental complexity that metal had always had. The multiple sections, the dynamic variation, the instrumental passages but delivered them with an urgency that arena metal had specifically engineered away.

The structural traits of the recombination follow the logic of what each system needs from the other. Hardcore bands introduced palm-muted riff-driven sections with greater tonal depth. The palm mute being the specific technique that allows a guitar to produce both rhythmic precision and low-end weight simultaneously. The technique that bridges the gap between hardcore's percussive attack and metal's physical density. Tempos fluctuated — slightly slower than peak hardcore velocity but heavier per strike, the decrease in speed more than compensated by the increase in physical impact. Breakdowns emerged as a structural element. The moment in a song where the tempo drops and the riff becomes the entire content, where rhythmic emphasis replaces pure velocity and the weight of the music becomes its primary expressive tool. Metal bands adopted shorter song structures and rawer production not because they had abandoned their technical ambitions but because the hardcore influence had demonstrated that compression was not the enemy of complexity but its most effective delivery mechanism.

The counterargument is that thrash metal evolved

primarily from NWOBHM influence rather than from hardcore, and that the crossover is overstated. That the two scenes remain separated with different audiences and different infrastructures and that the merger is a retrospective narrative imposed on what were actually parallel developments.

There is partial truth in this. The NWOBHM influence on Bay Area thrash is real, direct, and well-documented. Metallica's debt to Diamond Head and Iron Maiden is audible in ways that their debt to Minor Threat is not. The lineages are not equivalent.

But examine the shared infrastructure more carefully. Bay Area thrash shows in the early 1980's shared bills with punk and hardcore acts regularly. The audience demographics blended in ways that the labels' genre categories didn't reflect. The same people going to see Dead Kennedys were going to see early Metallica. Not because they had decided to experience a genre fusion but because both bands were playing the same venues on the same circuits. The rhythmic attack of early thrash — the tight, percussive downstroke riffing, the absence of the swing that British metal had retained from its blues inheritance reflects hardcore's rhythmic compression as directly as it reflects any British metal precedent. The production aesthetic of the early thrash recordings — raw, deliberately unglamorous — is not the NWOBHM aesthetic. It is the hardcore aesthetic applied to metal instrumentation.

This is not linear inheritance. It is recombination under shared pressure. Two forms reaching the same conclusion from different directions at the same moment because they were operating under the same external conditions and had discovered complementary solutions to complementary problems.

Reinforcement through weight stabilized the system temporarily. It restored the volatility that speed saturation had exhausted. It gave the aggression a physical dimension that pure velocity couldn't provide. The difference between being hit fast and being hit hard, and the specific impact of being hit by both at once. It allowed the music to scale without structural collapse by adding a vertical dimension. — more force per note — to the horizontal dimension — more notes per second — that hardcore had maxed out.

But recombination always produces new fault lines along the seams of the fusion. The merger of hardcore's structural compression and metal's tonal weight created a form that was more powerful than either predecessor or more unstable than either predecessor. The hardcore audience that had followed the escalation through speed and militancy now faced a music that had reintroduced elements. The riff's mythic weight, the tonal density, the developmental complexity of songs that lasted more than a minute. Hardcore had specifically rejected this as the enemy's vocabulary. The metal audience that had followed the escalation through technical refinement now faced a music that had stripped the production polish and the arena spectacle and the mythic distance that metal had built its identity around.

Two audiences. One music. And the music pulling in both directions simultaneously.

Once metal and hardcore fuse — once the riff and the compression exist in the same song at the same time — the next question doesn't wait for an answer.

How heavy can this get before the seams split open again?

THRASH AS SYNTHESIS (1983–1986)

By 1983, the recombination had produced enough material to recognize itself as something new.

It didn't have a stable name yet. The press was still reaching for vocabulary — speed metal, power metal, the crossover — categories that described individual attributes of the thing without capturing what the thing actually was. But the music knew what it was before the language did. The hardcore-metal fusion assembling itself through shared venue infrastructure and tape trading networks had reached the point of synthesis. The point at which the two source materials had been combined thoroughly enough is that the result was no longer audibly a combination of two things but a single coherent form with its own internal logic and its own developmental pressures.

That form was thrash metal. And thrash was the most complete musical synthesis the mutation cycle had yet produced.

The synthesis was not simply additive. Hardcore speed plus metal weight does not equal thrash any more than mixing two primary colors produces a third. What thrash produced was different from either predecessor because the combination had generated properties that neither source material contained. The riffs carried both the percussive aggression of hardcore's rhythmic attack and the tonal density of metal's low-end weight. The combination produced a physical impact that exceeded the sum of its components. The songs maintained hardcore's structural compression while developing the internal complexity that metal's multiple-section architecture allowed. A form that could deliver maximum intensity across five or six minutes without the energy dissipating. Pure hardcore couldn't do that because brevity was its only tool. Pure metal couldn't do it because its arena-optimized structures had been engineered to build slowly toward spectacle rather than sustain urgency continuously.

The geography of synthesis matters. The Bay Area was not an accident. San Francisco and its surrounding cities contained a concentration of venues, rehearsal spaces, record stores, and radio stations — particularly KFJC and Maximum Rocknroll's network. That created the conditions for cross-pollination between scenes that would have remained separate in cities with less concentrated infrastructure. The Keystone in Berkeley. The Stone in San Francisco. The Mabuhay Gardens, which had been the center of the Bay Area punk scene since the late 1970s and whose audience had grown up ready for something that honored punk's structural lessons while demanding more than three chords could offer. These rooms were small enough to preserve the physical proximity that hardcore had established as non-negotiable. Large enough to accommodate the sonic density that metal's tonal weight required.

Kill 'Em All in 1983 is the document that marks the synthesis becoming conscious. The record carries every element of the recombination in its final resolved form. The NWOBHM dual-guitar architecture compressed into hardcore brevity, the technical precision of metal's instrumental tradition applied to rhythmic patterns that owed their aggression to hardcore's percussive attack. Production raw enough to feel honest without being so minimal that it collapsed the low-end weight distinguishing the form from pure hardcore. The songs developed. They had sections. They had dynamic variation. There were not ninety-second bursts of maximum intensity. But they delivered their content with an urgency and physical directness that arena metal had lost and hardcore had been the only available model for recovering.

Haunting the Chapel in 1984 and Hell Awaits in 1985 pushed the synthesis toward its extreme edge. Where Metallica resolved the tension between hardcore compression and metal complexity toward development — longer songs, more intricate arrangements, technical ambition as a primary value. Slayer resolved it toward intensity. The tempos stayed closer to the hardcore ceiling. The production stayed raw. The tonal darkness went further into dissonance than Metallica's more conventionally musical approach would allow. Slayer made explicit the mythic darkness that thrash had mostly kept implicit. The occult imagery, the inverted structures, the deliberate offense. In doing so identified the boundary of the form's mainstream accessibility while also defining its extreme potential.

The audience thrash generated was the most noteworthy evidence of the synthesis's success. Kids who had come through hardcore brought physical engagement, DIY values, the anti-hierarchy instinct. Kids who had come through metal brought technical appreciation, the album-oriented listening, the willingness to follow a band through multiple records of increasing complexity. The blended audience was more diverse in its expectations than either source community. That diversity was both the form's greatest strength and the source of its next instability.

Thrash had solved the recombination problem so completely that it immediately began generating the pressures of its own success.

The technical escalation thrash initiated was self-reinforcing in a way that would have been familiar from the arena metal playbook. Once Metallica established a technical baseline with Kill 'Em All, the next record had to develop beyond it. Once Slayer established an intensity baseline with Hell Awaits, the next record had to exceed it. The escalation ladder that punk had rejected and hardcore had temporarily dismantled was being rebuilt inside thrash with the same structural logic. A faster, more complex, more extreme version. The same version that had made arena metal inaccessible in the first place. The ladder was lower. But it was rising.

The audience split that technical escalation produced was the clearest sign that thrash had created a ceiling of its own. On one side: the audience followed the escalation upward, wanting more speed, more complexity, more extremity. This audience would eventually generate death metal, black metal, and the extreme forms that treated thrash's ceiling as a floor. On the other hand: the audience that wanted to stay at the level of accessibility thrash initially achieved. The aggression and the energy and the physical impact without following the escalation into territory that required significant prior knowledge to navigate. This audience was sitting directly in the path of the commercial infrastructure that had been watching thrash develop from a distance and was now beginning to calculate its revenue potential.

That calculation was not wrong. Thrash had produced something genuinely powerful and genuinely accessible. More accessible than hardcore had ever been because it retained the song structures and musical complexity that allowed listeners without hardcore backgrounds to engage with it. The major labels that had co-opted punk's energy in the late 1970s were running the same calculation on thrash. It produced the same answer it always produces - sign the most accessible acts, smooth production, widen the audience, extract the revenue.

Master of Puppets in 1986 marked both the apex of thrash as a pure form and the beginning of its institutional absorption. The record was thrash's most complete artistic achievement. The synthesis fully realized, the balance between hardcore urgency and metal complexity held at its most precise and most powerful. It was also a record made with a production budget and label infrastructure that the DIY networks of three years earlier couldn't have supported. The ladder had risen. The walls were beginning to build.

Below those walls, two things were happening simultaneously. The audience being locked out of thrash's escalating technical hierarchy by kids who wanted aggression. They desired its energy but not the complexity for whom thrash was already beginning to feel like it required credentials to access. Thrash's physical impact without thrash's technical demands. And the hardcore veterans who had followed the recombination into thrash but never fully abandoned punk's structural principles were beginning to feel the same dissatisfaction that punk had felt toward arena metal a decade earlier. The music was good. Genuinely great. But it started to belong to the people who could play it rather than the people who needed it.

Those two audiences — locked out at the bottom, alienated at the top — were the seeds of the next mutation. They didn't know each other yet. Different rooms, different cities, different vocabularies for describing what they wanted. But they wanted the same thing: impact without the hierarchy, weight without the distance, the aggression without the credential.

Chapter 5 has traced a single escalation arc across four stages — speed, militancy, weight, synthesis — because the arc was continuous rather than episodic. Each stage produced the conditions for the next with the same structural logic. Punk's access created the conditions for hardcore's escalation. Hardcore's escalation created the conditions for metal's reentry. Metal's reentry created the conditions for the synthesis that thrash represented.

The synthesis is not the end of the story. It is the establishment of a new baseline — a new set of conditions that the next generation of musicians and audiences would inherit and mutate in response. Thrash gave the mutation cycle the most sophisticated and powerful form it had yet produced. It also gave the cycle its most clearly defined new ceiling. Its most legible new invitation for the correction.

The people standing outside them were already looking for materials.

CHAPTER SIX

When the Center Could Not Hold

MUTATION WITHOUT A CENTER (1984–1989)

Hardcore maxed speed. Metal regained weight. Now the borders are dissolving. Not because anyone decided they should but because the pressure on both sides had built to the point where the border itself became the obstacle.

By the mid-1980s, both systems had stabilized into their own internal logic in ways that were beginning to replicate the problem each had originally been a response. Hardcore had solved punk's diffusion by hardening its identity. The behavioral codes, the visual vocabulary, the scene infrastructure. In hardening it had created the narrowness that always follows when a community defines its borders too precisely. The music was as fast as it could get. The ideology was as tight as it could get. The scene was as internally coherent as it could get. And internal coherence, taken far enough, becomes a closed system. Closed systems don't mutate. They calcify.

Thrash had solved the hardcore-metal recombination problem with genuine brilliance and was now generating a technical escalation that was beginning to rebuild the hierarchy hardcore dismantled. The ladder was lower than the arena metal ladder had been. But it was rising with the same structural logic — faster, more complex, more technically demanding. The audience at the bottom was beginning to feel the same exclusion that had generated punk in the first place.

Two systems. Two ceilings. Same structural problem.

Crossbreeding becomes inevitable not as an aesthetic preference but as the structural consequence of two forms reaching their limits in adjacent spaces.

The Age of Quarrel in 1986 is the document that makes hybridization audible as a completed thing rather than a work in progress. Formed from the same CBGB infrastructure that had generated New York hardcore, the Cro-Mags brought a guitar tone and riff vocabulary that had no precedent in pure hardcore. The palm-muted precision of the riffing was metal. The delivery, the tempos, the structural directness were hardcore. The breakdown sections anchoring the songs. The moments where the tempo dropped and the riff became the entire content. Where weight replaced velocity as the primary expressive tool were neither metal nor hardcore exclusively. They were something the fusion had generated that neither source material contained. The Age of Quarrel didn't sound like a genre experiment. It sounded like a form that had found itself.

The same recombination was happening simultaneously in cities with no direct connection to New York and no coordinated relationship with each other. In Texas, Dirty Rotten Imbeciles were accelerating thrash's technical riffing while retaining hardcore's structural brevity. The songs are short enough to honor punk's anti-indulgence principle. The guitar work complex enough to demand focused attention that pure hardcore had never required. In Boston, Agnostic Front had thickened their tonal attack and tightened their rhythmic precision into something sitting at the intersection of hardcore's confrontational directness and metal's physical density. In Cleveland by the late 1980s, Integrity was injecting tonal darkness and metallic dissonance into hardcore frameworks that pointed toward a register the original movement had specifically avoided. The mythic dread, the atmospheric weight demonstrating that punk's rejection of atmosphere had been a tactical decision rather than a permanent one.

Regional experiments were multiplying faster than any centralized authority could track or contain. And this is the shift that defines the chapter — the shift that makes everything that follows structurally different from everything that came before.

In the 1970s, Birmingham formalized heaviness. One city, one scene, one set of conditions producing a mutation that spread outward from a single point. In 1977, London and New York anchored punk — two cities developing in parallel, still identifiable as the nodes through which the mutation's logic flowed. In the early 1980s, hardcore had identifiable hubs. D.C., Los Angeles, Boston — cities where the scene's identity was being defined with enough clarity that other cities could orient themselves in relation to it. The mutation had a center. The center had authority. The authority had consequences.

By 1986, crossover had no center. The mutation was happening everywhere simultaneously and everywhere was developing its own version without reference to a dominant model.

The mechanism that made immediate decentralized mutation possible was the tape trading network. A global infrastructure of cassette duplication and postal exchange. It had been building since the early hardcore days and had reached sufficient density by the mid-1980s. Its function is as a genuine alternative distribution system for music that the commercial infrastructure had no interest in and no mechanism for handling.

A band recording a demo on a four-track in a rehearsal space in Tampa could have that recording in the hands of a musician in Birmingham within weeks. The address lists maintained in zine back pages, the trade agreements negotiated through handwritten letters, the padded envelopes moving across continents. This compressed the evolutionary timeline of musical mutation in ways that had no precedent in the history of heavy music. Birmingham had been able to anchor heaviness in 1970 partly because the speed of information transfer meant that what Birmingham was doing took time to reach other cities. Time allowed the mutation to develop a stable identity before it encountered competing mutations. By the mid-1980s, that time had collapsed entirely. Scenes were borrowing from each other before either had fully developed, which meant the borrowing was built into the development rather than applied after the fact.

DIY labels pressed small runs — hundreds of copies rather than thousands, distributed through the same postal networks that moved the tapes, sold at shows and through zine advertisements rather than through retail channels that required commercial viability to access. The economic barriers to releasing music had dropped to the point where a band needed only enough money to press the record and enough addresses to know where to send it. No label infrastructure. No radio promotion. No retail distribution. Just the network, which was dense enough and motivated enough to do all those things at a fraction of the cost.

The structural consequences of the recombination followed the logic of what each system was contributing to the hybrid. Metallic riff complexity layered onto hardcore tempos produced a rhythmic density that neither source material could generate alone. The riff carrying harmonic and tonal information that pure hardcore's minimal chord vocabulary couldn't produce. The tempo carried the urgency and physical impact that metal's arena-optimized structures had engineered away. Breakdowns formalized as expected song architecture. No longer spontaneous moments of rhythmic emphasis but deliberate structural elements the audience anticipated and the musicians built toward. The breakdown functions as the song's primary emotional and physical event rather than a deviation from the main argument. Gang vocals combined with palm-muted precision created a specific social texture that neither metal nor hardcore had previously achieved. The collective voice of the hardcore tradition carried on top of the technical instrument work of the metal tradition. The result sounded both intimate and crushing.

Production stayed raw because raw production was both an ideological commitment and a practical necessity. The scenes didn't have the budget for studio polish and didn't want it even when they could have accessed it. But raw production in 1986 crossover was rhythmically tighter than raw production in 1976 punk had been. The music required a precision the earlier rawness didn't demand. You no longer needed arena polish. But you needed tighter hands than three chords and two minutes had required.

Access remained possible. The economic barriers stayed low. The DIY infrastructure stayed intact. But skill had re-entered the equation quietly and without announcement. Not the virtuoso credentialism of arena metal, not the deliberate anti-skill ideology of early punk, but a functional precision that the music required and that anyone willing to put in the rehearsal time could develop. The ladder was low. But it was there again.

The crossing wasn't a genre experiment. It was the logical next move available to musicians who had reached the ceiling of both source forms and needed somewhere to go. You couldn't play faster. You could play more precisely. You couldn't get heavier in the purely tonal sense without a production budget the DIY infrastructure couldn't support. You could get more rhythmically complex, more structurally varied, more deliberate about how the weight was deployed within the song rather than simply how much weight the song contained.

The social infrastructure accelerated what musical logic had made inevitable. Hardcore kids were listening to thrash because thrash was the most intense music available that still had songs. Metal kids were attending hardcore shows because hardcore had physical immediacy and audience proximity that the arena circuit had eliminated from metal. The tape trading networks were moving recordings across genre boundaries as freely as they moved them across geographic ones. The pit at a crossover show in New York in 1986 contained people who had come through hardcore and people who had come through metal and people who had come through neither. They were just there because someone had told them it was the most intense thing happening in the city. The pit didn't care about genre labels because the pit was a physical experience and physical experience operates below the level at which genre labels have authority.

The counterargument is that crossover was commercially marginal. That thrash and mainstream metal still dominated the larger markets. That the hybrids being developed in New York and Texas and Boston and Cleveland were niche experiments with limited influence on the broader development of heavy music. That is commercially accurate. And it is analytically irrelevant.

Mutation doesn't begin at scale. It begins at stress points. In the places where the existing system's contradictions are most visible and the pressure to resolve them is most acute. Crossover scenes operated under maximum friction. Small budgets that forced creative economy. Volatile crowds that provided immediate feedback on whether the music was working. Dense touring networks that put bands in front of new audiences constantly and forced rapid adaptation. The commercial mainstream was insulated from those pressures by the infrastructure of label investment and radio promotion. The crossover underground had nothing but those pressures. Friction accelerates change. The scenes that were commercially marginal in 1986 were evolutionary. The places where the next mutations were being assembled before the mainstream had any awareness that assembly was occurring.

If thrash had fully absorbed hardcore's energy without retaining the technical hierarchy its escalation was generating — if it had found a way to maintain the urgency and rawness at a level of complexity that didn't require years of development to access — the hybrid lane might never have opened. If hardcore had simultaneously rejected the metallic riffing entering its vocabulary — had maintained three-chord minimalism as a non-negotiable principle rather than a starting point — the two systems might have continued their parallel development without the overlap that generated the recombination.

Instead, the recombination spread because no centralized authority existed to contain it. No label had defined crossover as a genre with requirements. No magazine had canonized a crossover canon that established which bands were legitimate and which were experiments. No single city owned the mutation's identity the way Birmingham had owned heaviness or D.C. had owned straight edge. The system was decentralized — genuinely, structurally, irreversibly decentralized in a way that no previous phase of the mutation cycle had been.

Decentralization increases volatility because it removes the stabilizing function that centralized authority has always performed. When Birmingham defined heaviness, other cities could orient themselves in relation to Birmingham's definition. When D.C. defined straight edge, other scenes could accept or reject D.C.'s definition. Definitions provide stability even for the people who reject them. You know what you're pushing against. When no center exists, there is nothing to push against and nothing to orient in relation to. Every band is making its own decisions about what the music should be, and every band's decision feeds back into the network and influence every other band's decision. The result is a system in permanent motion with no equilibrium point.

When no one controls mutation, acceleration multiplies. The next phase won't just be heavier. It will be structurally unstable by design. Not because anyone chose instability but because the infrastructure that had made stability possible had been replaced by something that ran on volatility as its primary fuel.

EXTREMITY ARMS RACE (1987–1990)

Crossover removed the borders. Now the absence of borders becomes its own kind of pressure.

When no authority defines the ceiling, the ceiling disappears. And when the ceiling disappears, the question of how far the music can go stops being theoretical and becomes a practical competition with no agreed endpoint. By the late 1980's, hardcore-metal hybrids were everywhere simultaneously. In Florida and California and the UK and Scandinavia and Brazil, connected by tape trading networks that moved recordings across continents in weeks and zine networks that named and described and debated what was happening before any commercial infrastructure had noticed it was happening at all. The mutations were developing in parallel without any single node having the authority to declare what the form was or where its limits were.

When no authority defines the ceiling, bands test it. Not because assessing the ceiling is a conscious ideology but because distinction is survival in a system with no gatekeepers. In a centralized system, the gatekeeper tells you whether your music is acceptable. In a decentralized system, the network tells you whether your music is interesting. And interesting, in a network running on escalation, means further than what came before. Extremity becomes the currency of visibility. The bands that push furthest get talked about most. The demos that arrive from furthest outside the existing envelope get traded most aggressively. The system rewards escalation because sameness disappears into noise and extremity is the only reliable way to remain audible.

Reign in Blood in 1986 reset the ceiling so completely that every band operating in the extreme underground had to recalibrate its position relative to it. Twenty-nine minutes. Ten songs. No groove in the traditional sense. All replaced by a relentless percussive attack that Dave Lombardo sustained at tempos that made the surrounding thrash scene sound measured by comparison. Tom Araya's vocals delivered without the melodic concession that even the most aggressive metal had retained. Kerry King and Jeff Hanneman operating at the intersection of technical precision and tonal violence. Treating conflict not as a device but as the fundamental language of the record. Reign in Blood didn't feel like a thrash record that had been pushed further. It felt like a different kind of object — compressed to the point where the compression itself became the expressive content. Rick Rubin's production, clean and brutal at once, gave the record a clarity that made its extremity more rather than less disturbing. You could hear exactly what was happening. What was happening was the most aggressive thing that had yet been committed to a major label release.

In the UK the following year, Napalm Death detonated the speed ceiling from a different direction entirely. Scum in 1987 didn't approach the ceiling and push through it. It treated the ceiling as irrelevant. Songs collapsed toward seconds — not minutes, seconds. The blast beat drumming that Mick Harris developed on Scum was not an acceleration of existing punk or hardcore patterns. It was a different relationship between the drummer and time entirely. The snare and bass drum alternating at speeds that made individual beats inaudible as individual beats. The rhythm is becoming texture rather than pulse. Riff fragments replaced full structures because full structures required time the songs didn't have. The result sounded less like music being played very fast and more like music being used as a weapon. Not the controlled aggression of Black Flag or Minor Threat but something closer to pure sonic force delivered without apology or structure.

In Florida, Morbid Angel were moving in a third direction at the same time. Where Slayer compressed and Napalm Death atomized, Morbid Angel expanded. It sank downward, into lower tunings and darker harmonic language. A riff architecture of genuine complexity that treated the extreme metal framework as a vehicle for musical ideas. This form had not previously been asked to carry such weight. Trey Azagthoth's guitar work on the demos circulating through the tape trading network in the mid-to-late 1980s operated at the intersection of technical sophistication and genuine evil in a way that made the surrounding scene's extremity feel comparatively candid. It was structural — built into the intervals, the tunings, the rhythmic displacement that made the riffs feel precise and subverting.

Three regions. Three different intensification variables. Three different answers to the question of how much further the music could go. All three developing, aware of each other through the tape network, each one's existence accelerating the others' climb.

The structural consequences spread across every available variable. Not because anyone coordinated the escalation but because the tape network made every escalation immediately visible to every other scene. Visibility in a system running on division created pressure to respond in kind or exceed.

Tempo increased beyond thrash norms through the arrangement of the blast beat as a standard technique. What Harris had deployed on Scum as an extreme gesture became, within two years, a foundational element of the grindcore and early death metal vocabulary. A technique that dozens of drummers were learning because the network had demonstrated that it was possible and the escalation logic demanded that techniques be deployed. Song length forked in a way that reflected the two dominant strategies for maximizing energy density. Ultra-short songs in the grindcore tradition, which treated shortness as the most efficient delivery mechanism. A maximum impact per second and extended but denser compositions in the death metal tradition. It treated duration as an opportunity for structural difficulty that rewarded repeated listening. Two opposite responses to the same pressure, which is why they coexisted without contradiction in a system that had no authority to declare one correct.

Tuning dropped lower because lower tuning produces more low-end physical presence with less technical modification. A down-tuned guitar delivers a tonal weight that standard tuning requires additional amplification and production investment to replicate. In a scene running on minimal budgets and raw production, down-tuning was the most economically efficient way to increase physical impact. It was also sonically distinctive. The low tunings Florida death metal bands were developing by the late 1980's produced a harmonic language audibly different from anything the thrash or hardcore traditions had established. Which made it immediately identifiable on a tape trading network where sonic distinction was the primary currency of attention.

Riff complexity intensified as competition between scenes created pressure for musical distinction that pure speed and pure weight could no longer provide alone. Once every band was playing fast and heavy, the bands that wanted to stand out had to play fast and heavy and interesting. This required compositional sophistication that the extreme metal tradition was developing with increasing speed and increasing technical demand. The return of riff density to the extreme underground was not a return to arena metal's values. It was a development of the recombination's logic to its next available escalation point.

Vocals abandoned fluency for texture because fluency had become optional in a context where the physical experience of the music was the primary content. The death growl, the black metal shriek, the grindcore bark. Each treated the voice as an additional instrument in the sonic assault rather than a vehicle for lyrical communication. The words were still there, still carrying meaning for listeners who sought them out in lyric sheets. The vocal delivery had been optimized for impact rather than transmission. This was not laziness. It was a deliberate ranking of sonic density over semantic clarity. The recognition that in music operating at these extremes, the body receives the content before the mind does.

The arms race follows from the structure of the network that enabled it. Recombination removes genre borders. Removing genre borders removes the definitions that tell bands where the ceiling is. Removing the ceiling makes the ceiling a competitive variable. Making the ceiling competitive in a globally networked system means that every local escalation becomes a challenge to every other scene. A band in Birmingham hears a band in Tampa within weeks of the Tampa band recording the demo. If Tampa is faster, Birmingham has two options — match the speed or find a different variable to escalate. If Birmingham matches the speed, Tampa finds a different variable. The system generates escalation because the network makes every escalation visible. Visibility in a distinction-based economy creates pressure to respond.

This is not metaphor. It is the literal mechanism of how grindcore and death metal and proto-black metal developed simultaneously in geographically separated scenes without central coordination. Each aware of the others through the tape network. Each responding to the others' escalations with escalations of their own. The result being a competitive acceleration that no single scene controlled and no single scene could have produced alone.

The counterargument is that extremity was artistic exploration rather than competitive escalation. That the musicians developing grindcore and death metal were chasing genuine expression. A genuine artistic vision, genuine engagement with darkness and complexity. Reducing their work to a competitive arms race misses the authenticity that motivated it.

This deserves a direct response. Chuck Schuldiner of Death was genuinely trying to develop a musical language adequate to the darkness he was exploring. Azagthoth was genuinely pursuing a compositional vision of genuine sophistication. The members of Napalm Death were genuinely committed to a political and sonic radicalism that had nothing to do with outflanking competitors. The artistic motivation was real.

But expression and escalation are not opposite. They are, in the context of a decentralized network running on distinction, the same thing. The artistic impulse to push further, to find the form that most completely expresses the vision, to refuse the compromises that accessibility demands. These impulses are genuine and they produce escalation as their natural consequence. The arms race is not cynical. It is the structural form that sincere artistic ambition takes in a system where visibility requires distinction and distinction requires escalation. The musicians weren't chasing extremity for their own sake. They were chasing their vision with the full force of their ability. The system rewarded the ones who went furthest because furthest was what the network could most clearly see.

If crossover had stabilized into a balanced hybrid — moderate speed, moderate complexity, the kind of accessible middle ground that commercial logic would have preferred. Then extreme metal might have remained isolated niche experimentation. Without the global tape networks compressing the evolutionary timeline, without the competitive awareness the network created, regional scenes might have developed more slowly and in greater isolation. The Florida death metal scene might not have known what the UK grindcore scene was doing. The Norwegian proto-black metal scene might not have had access to the full range of extremity the tape network had assembled. Without awareness of competitors, the escalation would have cooled. Not because the artistic impulse would have disappeared but because the pressure accelerating its development would have been absent.

Instead, decentralization fueled comparison. No one controlled the mutation, so everyone pushed. Hardcore's speed and metal's weight and thrash's precision all intensified in different combinations in different regions. Each rise visible to every other region through the network, each visibility creating pressure for response.

The instability this produced was not the instability of a system about to collapse. It was the instability of a system running faster than any stabilizing mechanism could match. When extremity escalates unchecked, accessibility drops as a direct consequence. Participation narrows because the skills required to make this music — not just listen to it but make it — become increasingly specialized. Scenes tighten around the specific sub-genre they've developed because the sub-genre's specific demands create communities of shared expertise that outsiders can't easily enter.

The arms race doesn't just create heavier music. It fragments the system into sub-genres defined by how far they push a single variable — speed in grindcore, tonal darkness in death metal, atmospheric ideology in the proto-black metal developing in Scandinavia. Each sub-genre becomes increasingly self-referential, increasingly defined by its internal escalation rather than its relationship to any external context. Increasingly inaccessible to anyone who hasn't followed the escalation from its beginning.

And the more inaccessible the underground becomes, the more visible the distance between it and the surface grows. The surface, in the late 1980s, was not sitting still. While the underground was fragmenting into competing extremities, the mainstream was doing something entirely different. Something that the underground had declared irrelevant, but that millions of people were consuming with genuine enthusiasm. The next mutation won't come from pushing the extremity further. It will come from atmosphere returning.

Not the slow cosmic dread of early Sabbath. Not the militant confrontation of hardcore, but something colder and darker and more deliberately alienating than either. Something that had been watching the arms race from Scandinavia and had decided that the most extreme thing available was not speed or weight or brutality but a specific and total rejection of everything the mainstream had decided music was for.

The arms race created the conditions. The atmosphere would supply the answer.

UNDERGROUND INFRASTRUCTURE EXPLOSION

Extremity escalates. The delivery system mutates to carry it.

The fragmentation the arms race had produced created a distribution problem that the existing infrastructure had no mechanism for solving. By the mid-to-late 1980s, heavy music had splintered into crossover, thrash, early death metal, grindcore, and the proto-black metal assembling itself in Scandinavia with deliberate isolation from the rest of the underground's escalation logic. No major label fully controlled any of these forms. Too extreme, too commercially marginal, too deliberately inaccessible to attract the investment that would have brought label infrastructure with it. No mainstream press could track the fragmentation with sufficient speed or hardness to serve as a reliable guide. Arena circuits were not just irrelevant to these scenes. They were structurally incompatible. A grindcore band playing thirty-second songs to an audience that wanted physical confrontation at close range had no use for a 15,000-seat venue and no pathway into the routing system that filled one.

But fragmentation without connection is just isolation. And isolation slows mutation rather than accelerating it. The scenes needed to find each other.

The answer to the underground was not elegant. It was not efficient by any commercial standard. It was a global network of photocopied paper and padded envelopes and handwritten address lists that operated entirely outside the commercial infrastructure and moved faster than the commercial infrastructure could have believed possible for something with no budget and no central coordination.

Zines were the connective tissue. Not professionally printed magazines with advertising budgets and editorial hierarchies. Photocopied sheets folded and stapled in someone's bedroom and produced for the cost of paper. This distributed through the back pages of other zines where writers traded addresses with the same casual generosity that made the whole network function. A zine produced in a Stockholm suburb could reach a reader in São Paulo within weeks if the address were in the right list. The writing in those zines — reviews of demos, interviews conducted by mail, scene reports from cities that Kerrang! had never mentioned. It constituted a global critical infrastructure for music the mainstream press had no framework for understanding and no interest in developing.

The cassette demo was the fuel the zine infrastructure carried. A band recording in a garage in Tampa on a four-track could duplicate that recording for the cost of blank tapes and mail copies to addresses collected from zine back pages.

The person who received the tape would copy it for their own network. The copies would be copied again. A single demo recording could reach hundreds of listeners across multiple continents within months of its creation. None of those copies pass through any commercial channel. None of them generating revenue for anyone, all of them generating the awareness and comparative pressure that drove the escalation forward.

The specific human texture of this network matters because it reveals the mechanism. Consider Tomas Lindberg of At the Gates in Gothenburg, Sweden in 1988. A teenager with a list of addresses and a collection of tapes that had arrived from Florida and New York and Birmingham through the mail. Each one representing a scene he had never visited and musicians he had never met. Each one expanding his understanding of what the music could be and raising his internal standard for what his own band needed to achieve. The tape from Death or Morbid Angel or Napalm Death didn't arrive with commercial context or critical framing. It arrived as raw sound, evaluated purely on its own terms, and it arrived in direct competition with every other tape in the collection. That competitive awareness — the knowledge of exactly how far the music had already gone in other rooms on other continents — was the pressure that produced the Swedish death metal scene's specific combination of melodic sophistication and extreme aggression. The scene didn't develop in isolation. It developed in direct conversation with a global network it had never physically entered.

Tape trading became evolutionary fuel because it collapsed

the geographic isolation that had previously allowed scenes to develop at their own pace. It bypassed radio entirely. Not as an ideological gesture but as a practical necessity. No radio station was playing this music, and the network didn't need radio to function. Distribution costs dropped to the price of a blank cassette and a stamp. Gatekeeping weakened to the point of irrelevance. There was no gatekeeper between a band's four-track and a listener's tape deck. Mutation no longer needed permission. It no longer needed geography. It needed only a list of addresses and the willingness to fill envelopes.

The structural consequences follow the logic of what the network did to the evolutionary timeline.

Stylistic diffusion accelerated across continents in ways that had no model. The Birmingham mutation of 1970 had taken years to reach American audiences. The records had to be manufactured, distributed, stocked in stores, reviewed in magazines, and heard on radio before the sound could influence musicians in other cities. By the late 1980s, that process had been compressed to weeks. A scene developing in one city was aware of scenes developing on other continents before either had stabilized into a defined form. Which meant influences were absorbed during development rather than after it. The result was a hybridization that happened faster and more thoroughly than any previous phase of the mutation cycle. Bands absorbing distant influences not as finished products to be responded to but as works in progress to be incorporated into their own works in progress.

Scenes specialized while remaining connected. A paradox the tape network made structurally possible for the first time. The Florida death metal scene could develop its specific tonal language and rhythmic approach in sufficient depth to constitute a genuine regional identity while maintaining awareness of the UK grindcore scene and the Scandinavian proto-black metal scene and the New York crossover scene. Specialization and connection had previously been tense. The more specialized a scene became, the more it needed to isolate itself to maintain its identity. The tape network dissolved that tension by making connection costless. The specialization it enabled was therefore different from earlier phases — richer, more self-conscious, more capable of intentional development because the musicians knew exactly what they were specializing in relations.

Production stayed raw because the network's logic prioritized speed of exchange over fidelity of reproduction. A demo that sounded perfect but took six months to produce was less significant than a demo that sounded rough but arrived in circulation three months earlier. The arms race ran on information. It ran on the awareness of what other scenes were doing and the ability to respond. Raw production delivered that information faster. The rawness also was, as it had been in every previous phase of heavy music's development, an honest reflection of the resources available. Four-track recorders in rehearsal spaces. Minimal microphone placement. No mixing budget. The production sounded like what it was.

Extreme music in the late 1980s could not rely on the

corporate distribution pipelines built for arena stability. Those pipelines had been designed to move products that radio could play, and retail could stock and a mainstream audience could consume. Extreme metal was none of those things by design. The alternative was not to change the music to fit the pipeline. The alternative was to build a parallel pipeline that could carry the music as it was. And once that parallel pipeline existed — once the network of zines and tape trades and DIY labels and postal exchanges had reached sufficient density to function as a genuine distribution system — it created the conditions for the escalation.

Infrastructure and escalation fed each other in a recursive loop. Better infrastructure meant wider distribution. Wider distribution meant more competitive awareness. More competitive awareness meant more escalation. More escalation meant more music that needed the infrastructure to reach its audience. The loop ran faster with every cycle because each cycle added participants to the network and each new participant added their own address list and their own local scene's output to the system.

The counterargument is that underground networks existed long before the late 1980s extreme metal explosion. Punk had zines, hardcore had DIY labels, the infrastructure described here was a continuation of what those earlier movements had built rather than a genuine mutation in the delivery system itself. The Xeroxed fanzine and the self-released seven-inch were not inventions of the extreme metal underground. They inherited tools that the underground repurposed for its own requirements.

That is partially true. The tools were inherited. Without the punk and hardcore infrastructure that preceded it, the extreme metal network would have had to develop its distribution logic from scratch. Genealogy is real.

But scale changes impact in ways that make quantitative difference become qualitative difference. The punk zine network of 1977 connected scenes within cities and between a small number of cities already in cultural communication. The hardcore DIY network of the early 1980s expanded to reach a national level in the US and UK. The extreme metal tape trading network of the late 1980s was operating at a genuinely global level. With hundreds of bands on multiple continents trading simultaneously, cross-continental communication is dense enough to accelerate sub-genre classification in real time. Death metal in Florida. Grindcore in the UK. Proto-black metal in Scandinavia. Thrash variants in Brazil and Germany. Each of these regional developments was aware of the others within months of their emergence. Each awareness created the competitive pressure that drove the escalation. The escalation is driving the need for more awareness, the need for more awareness driving the expansion of the network.

No center. No hierarchy. Multiple scenes operating with equal authority and equal access to the network's resources. It worked like a web — Birmingham had been a single root from which everything else grew. London and New York in 1977 had been roots. D.C. and Los Angeles in the early 1980s had been roots. By 1989, the roots were gone. There were only connection points, each linked to multiple others, each capable of generating new growth in any direction without waiting for permission from anywhere else.

Without cheap cassette duplication — without affordable tape recorders and blank cassettes as mass market products — the extreme metal underground would have lacked its primary medium of exchange. Without affordable international postal rates, the geographic reach of the network would have been limited to national rather than international exchange. Regional sounds would have diverged more slowly because they would have developed in greater isolation. The Florida death metal scene would have known less about what the UK grindcore scene was doing and vice versa, and that reduced awareness would have cooled the competitive pressure that drove both scenes' escalation. The arms race requires contestants who know each other's positions. Without the infrastructure to communicate those positions globally, the race slows.

Instead, infrastructure intensified competition until the system reached a state with no precedent in the history of heavy music. The globally networked and locally independent at once. Every scene was developing its own specific identity with genuine regional depth. Every scene was also in constant communication with every other scene. The tension between local specificity and global awareness was not resolved. It was sustained as the system's primary generative condition. The source of both the specialization that gave each sub-genre its identity and the competitive escalation that drove each sub-genre to push further than it would have pushed in isolation.

This explosion does not stabilize the system. It removes the ceiling entirely — not by pushing through any specific ceiling but by eliminating the structural conditions that make ceilings possible. Ceilings exist when authority exists to enforce them. Authority exists when a center exists to generate it. Once the center was gone, the authority went with it. Without authority, there is no ceiling. Without a ceiling, acceleration becomes not just possible but the default state of a system that runs on distinction and rewards escalation.

The extreme underground of the late 1980s was the most volatile and most generative phase the mutation cycle had yet entered. It was also, by the logic of its own structure, the phase most completely immune to the kind of stabilization that would have made it commercially legible. Which meant that while it was generating the most intense music in the history of heavy music, the commercial mainstream was not watching. It was looking somewhere else entirely — at something brighter, louder in a unique way, more immediately accessible, and being delivered through a medium that the underground had no access to and no interest in.

The ceiling had been removed from the underground. The mainstream was building a new one.

NO CENTER HOLDS (1988–1992)

The underground explodes. The infrastructure globalizes. The extremity escalates past every previous ceiling. And then the center — the organizing principle that every previous phase of heavy music had relied on to give the mutation coherence and direction — simply ceases to exist.

This is not collapse. It needs to be understood clearly as something different from collapse, because the word collapse implies failure and what happened to heavy music's identity between 1988 and 1992 was not failure. It was the logical consequence of success. The success of the dispersed infrastructure in distributing mutation so efficiently and so globally that no single version of the mutation could accumulate enough authority to define what the form was supposed to be. The underground had built a system specifically designed to prevent centralization. The system worked. The prevention was total.

By the late 1980s, heavy music had no single dominant mutation path and the absence of dominance was structural rather than temporary. Thrash had peaked commercially. Master of Puppets in 1986 and The Black Album still ahead, but the creative ceiling of the form is already visible to anyone paying attention to what was developing below it. Hardcore had fractured along every fault line. Crossover had splintered into sub-scenes that shared infrastructure but not identity. The tape trading network connected everyone but connection without hierarchy removes the control that hierarchy had always provided. And control, it turned out, was what gave a musical form its readability.

When everything connects, nothing dominates. When nothing dominates, identity diffuses. When identity diffuses, the question of what heavy music is becomes unanswerable from inside the form.

In Tampa, Death was pushing the synthesis that Schuldiner had been developing since the mid-1980s toward a technical sophistication that was beginning to strain the death metal framework from the inside. Spiritual Healing in 1990 and Human in 1991 carried a compositional complexity — the guitar work increasingly intricate, the song structures increasingly developed, the production increasingly clear. That reflected genuine musical ambition rather than competitive escalation. Death was not trying to be more extreme than their peers. They were trying to be more complete. To build a form of heavy music that could carry the full weight of the musical ideas they were developing without constraint by the genre's ceiling. The death metal framework was expanding under the pressure of a musician who had outgrown the arms race and was building something more durable than any arms race could produce.

In Norway, Mayhem was doing the opposite with equal conviction and equal musical intelligence. The production philosophy that Euronymous was developing— intentionally degraded, lo-fi to the point of abstraction, the instruments bleeding into each other in a murk that made early Sabbath recordings sound clinical by comparison. This was not a failure of resources. It was an ideology of sound. The argument was that fidelity was a form of compromise, cleaning up production was a concession to accessibility, and accessibility was precisely what the music was designed to refuse. The atmosphere that the degraded production generated was not incidental. It was the content. Where death metal had moved toward clarity in its escalation of complexity, black metal moved toward obscurity. Not as a technical limitation but as a philosophical position about what music was for and who it was allowed to reach.

In Belo Horizonte, Sepultura were developing a form of heavy music with no direct equivalent anywhere else in the global network. A thrash density and rhythmic aggression filtered through a Brazilian musical sensibility that the tape trading network had never had to accommodate. The percussion vocabulary, the rhythmic complexity, the relationship between the heavy guitar attack and the specifically Brazilian rhythmic tradition underpinning it. These elements produced a sound that was recognized in conversation with the global extreme metal network and unlike anything the network had generated from its American or European nodes. Sepultura was the clearest demonstration that the decentralized infrastructure had succeeded in its most radical implication. That heavy music was no longer a form that originated in specific Western cities and spread outward. It was a global language that diverse cultures were now speaking with their own accents. While producing meanings the original speakers hadn't anticipated and couldn't have generated alone.

Three continents. Three completely different answers to the question of what the escalation required next. Death moving toward technical completion. Mayhem moving toward atmospheric extremity. Sepultura is moving toward rhythmic synthesis. And together, in dozens of other cities across the network. With grindcore compressing toward structural collapse in the UK, black metal developing its ideological framework in Scandinavia, thrash refining its precision in Germany and fragmenting into speed metal and power metal variants in the US, death metal establishing regional identities in Sweden and Finland distinct from the Florida model without being derived from any other single source.

Each sub-genre was pushing a different lever. Speed. Weight. Atmosphere. Complexity. Ideology. Regional identity. There was no longer a single heavy identity because the form had acquired too many identities for any one of them to achieve dominance. The mutation was no longer moving in a direction. It was moving in all directions at once.

The identity diffusion follows from the infrastructure the underground had built to survive without commercial support. The bottleneck that had allowed Birmingham to anchor heaviness in 1970 was an information bottleneck. The slowness of musical transmission meant that the mutation developing in one city had time to stabilize into a defined identity before it encountered competing mutations from other cities. Remove the bottleneck and remove the stabilization mechanism. The tape trading network had removed the bottleneck so completely that by 1990 no mutation had time to stabilize before it was already in conversation with competing mutations developing all together on other continents.

The progression from centralized to decentralized authority follows a clear structural logic. Birmingham in 1970 — one city, one scene, the mutation developing in near-isolation with sufficient time to establish a stable identity before the world heard it. London and New York in 1977 developing in parallel, still exercising sufficient authority over the form's definition to make other cities' punk scenes orient themselves in relation to the London or New York model. D.C. and Los Angeles in the early 1980s. Multiple nodes, but still sequential enough that straight edge ideology and L.A.'s hardcore infrastructure could each achieve genuine authority within the form before being challenged by competing definitions.

By 1990, the sequence had collapsed into simultaneity. No node dominated because the infrastructure had made dominance structurally impossible. The zine network had too many voices operating in too many directions for any single critical framework to achieve the kind of authority that Rolling Stone had exercised over rock in the 1970s or that Maximum Rocknroll had briefly exercised over hardcore in the early 1980s. No label set aesthetic boundaries because no label had signed enough of the significant extreme metal acts to have a commercial interest in defining the genre's limits. The scenes defined themselves internally, which meant each scene's definition was authoritative within its own network and irrelevant to every other scene's network.

The counterargument identifies something real — that even in the early 1990s, certain hubs were clearly influential. Florida death metal had generated the form's foundational documents and its foundational bands, and its influence on death metal scenes in Sweden and Finland and Germany was genuine and traceable. Norwegian black metal was developing an ideology and an aesthetic that would define a global sub-genre for decades. The influence was real. The hubs existed.

But the hubs were together rather than in sequence, and that simultaneity is the distinction that changes everything. Every previous phase of heavy music's development had been characterized by sequential dominance. One city or scene establishing authority and then being challenged by another. The challenge eventually displaces the original and establishing a new center. Birmingham displaced the blues-rock model. London and New York challenged arena rock's dominance. D.C. and Los Angeles defined hardcore's parameters before those parameters fragmented. In each case, the sequence was legible. You could trace the line of authority from one center to the next and understand the mutation as a directed process with identifiable turning points.

By 1990, there was no sequence. Florida death metal and Norwegian black metal and Brazilian thrash and UK grindcore and Swedish melodic death metal were all developing. Each influencing the others through the network, none achieving the kind of authority that would have allowed it to define the form's direction. Influence flowed in multiple directions at once. Scenes competed and coexisted rather than replacing one another. The form had no turning points because it had no single line to turn.

A major label signing the significant extreme metal acts across sub-genres in the late 1980s — standardizing one dominant strain, investing in its production and distribution, using the commercial infrastructure to amplify one version of the mutation above all others — could theoretically have recentralized the system. A unified extreme metal identity with controlled aesthetic boundaries, defined by the commercial interests of the label that had invested in it, distributed through the commercial channels the underground had bypassed. The form would have been legible. It would have been marketable. It would have been one thing rather than many.

It would also have been a different thing than what it was. One stripped of the regional specificity, the ideological diversity, the competitive escalation that the decentralized network had generated. No label made that consolidation because no label understood what was developing in time to consolidate it. By the time anyone with commercial resources was paying attention, the form had fragmented beyond the point where consolidation was structurally possible.

Instead, diffusion accelerated fragmentation. No center held because the infrastructure prevented consolidation, and as soon as any strain showed signs of stabilizing into a dominant form, the network's competitive logic generated escalations that pushed beyond it. The system's immune response to centralization was built into its architecture. Running on distinction rather than consensus, rewarding the bands that refused the stabilization rather than the bands that accepted it.

The instability in the identity diffusion produced was different in kind from every previous instability in heavy music's development. The earlier instabilities had been instabilities of form — the music was changing faster than the audience or the industry could track. The mutations were outrunning the categories that described them, the scenes were developing in directions the existing infrastructure wasn't built to carry. Those instabilities were resolved, eventually, by the emergence of new forms stable enough to generate new categories, new infrastructure, new centers of authority that could anchor the mutation long enough for it to become legible.

The instability of 1990 to 1992 was an instability of identity itself. The question of what heavy music was had become genuinely unanswerable. Not because no one was paying attention but because the form had become too many different things for any single answer to be accurate. Technical precision in Tampa. Lo-fi atmosphere in Oslo. Political grind in Birmingham. Militant hardcore-metal fusion in New York. Melodic death metal in Gothenburg. Rhythmic synthesis in Belo Horizonte. Each of these was heavy music. None of them was the definition of heavy music. The category expanded past the point where it could function as a category.

And that is the mutation. Not a new sound. Not a new technique. Not a new ideology. The mutation is the diffusion of identity itself. The moment when a form that had always had a center, however contested and however temporary, loses the center permanently and becomes instead a field of escalation with no throne and no canon and no dominant blueprint.

What this produced was not chaos, despite the appearance of chaos from outside. From inside the network, the field was legible. You knew where Florida death metal ended and Swedish melodic death metal began. You knew what Norwegian black metal's ideological commitments were and how they differed from UK grindcore's political commitments. You knew which demos were worth trading and which were derivatives. The field had internal structure. It just didn't have a center, and without a center it was invisible for anyone approaching it from outside without a guide.

The invisibility was consequential. While the extreme underground was generating the most diverse and most evolutionary phase of heavy music's development, the commercial mainstream had no mechanism for seeing it. The forms were too extreme, the production too raw, the distribution too far outside the commercial infrastructure for any of them to register as a cultural phenomenon rather than a subcultural curiosity. The mainstream was not watching the underground in 1990 and 1991. It was watching something else. Something that had been building its own momentum through an entirely different infrastructure. It aimed at an entirely different audience, optimized for an entirely different kind of visibility.

The underground and the mainstream had been diverging since thrash metal's commercial peak in the mid-1980's. By 1991 they were operating in such different registers — different economics, different aesthetics, different relationships to the audience, different ideas about what music was for. They barely constituted the same cultural phenomenon. The underground was running on escalation and distinction and the refusal of accessibility. The mainstream was running on spectacle and accessibility and the amplification of identity through a medium the underground had no access to and no interest in.

What heavy music was in 1991 depended entirely on where you were standing when you asked the question. From inside the underground, it was a field of competing extremities. No center, no canon, just the network and the escalation and the next envelope in the mail. From inside the mainstream, it was something else entirely. Something with bigger hair and brighter lights and an extremely specific relationship to a television channel that had changed the economics of music visibility more thoroughly than anything since the transistor radio.

The underground had removed the ceiling. The mainstream had built a new floor, higher and more visible than anything the underground could reach, and it was broadcasting from it twenty-four hours a day.

The next phase won't unify the two systems. It will drive them further apart — and then, from the distance between them, generate the collision that neither system saw coming.

Between 1984 and 1992, the extreme underground was the most generative and invisible period in the history of heavy music — an international network running on cassette tapes and photocopied paper, and one that was producing the form's most significant evolutionary developments, yet ensuring that such developments would be structurally inaccessible to anyone without a guide. While the underground removed every ceiling it encountered, the commercial mainstream was making something else entirely — a spectacle crafted for television, a structure optimized for a medium that traded in image as much as sound, financed with major label investment that comprehended the new economics of music visibility better than any earlier generation of industry infrastructure had. Chapter 7 looks at what that spectacle was, how it was constructed, and why the system that birthed it contained the seeds of its own demolition before the first video ever came to air.

CHAPTER SEVEN

When Heavy Reorganized

THE NEW CENTER (1983–1991)

The underground had removed every ceiling it encountered. By the early 1980s, heavy music was fragmenting faster than any centralized authority could track — thrash accelerating in the Bay Area, hardcore splintering regionally, death metal forming in Florida, grindcore detonating in the UK, tape networks connecting all of it globally without corporate mediation. No center held. No single city owned the mutation. No label defined the form. The system was running on volatility as its primary fuel and producing the most evolutionary significant music in the history of the form as a direct consequence.

And while all of that was happening, a television channel changed everything.

MTV launched in August 1981 and spent approximately two years becoming the most powerful gatekeeping mechanism in the history of popular music. Not radio. Not the record store. Not the live circuit. Television — a medium that transmitted image and sound that reached into living rooms across the country through the cable infrastructure expanding household by household through the early 1980's. That created a new kind of music discovery in which the audience didn't seek out the music but sat in front of a screen and let the music come to them. The indifference of the consumption model was not a bug. It was the feature that made MTV's gatekeeping power an absolute. Radio required the listener to tune in and stay tuned. MTV required only that the television be on.

The implications for heavy music were structural and immediate. The form that had spent the previous decade developing its identity through physical infrastructure. The live show, the record store, the touring circuit, the gradual accumulation of audience through presence and volume and confrontational directness. This was now operating in a media environment. A physical infrastructure that had been supplemented by a visual economy that operated according to entirely different selection criteria. MTV didn't care how loud you were. It cared how you looked.

The underground couldn't satisfy that criteria and didn't try. Blast beats don't translate to broadcast compression. Lo-fi production collapses on television speakers optimized for speech clarity. Militancy complicates advertiser relationships. Ideological density resists the three-minute single format that MTV's programming logic demanded. The extreme underground was building the most intense music the form had ever generated through the infrastructure of tape trading, zine networks, DIY labels, club circuits. A system designed to bypass the commercial channels MTV represented. The two systems were not in competition. They were operating in different dimensions entirely, each invisible to the other, each running on incompatible logic.

Which left a vacuum at the commercial center of heavy music that major labels recognized before anyone else did.

The vacuum was specific. Heavy music had proven its commercial viability through the arena rock era. The Priest and Iron Maiden and Def Leppard tours of the late 1970s and early 1980s had demonstrated that a heavy audience existed at scale and would pay arena prices to access it. That audience hadn't disappeared. It had simply lost its commercial center when arena metal's momentum stalled. The underground fragmented into forms too extreme for mainstream consumption. The major label calculation was straightforward — find a form of heaviness that retained enough of the genre's sonic identity to satisfy the existing heavy audience while meeting MTV's visual and structural requirements. Find the heaviness that could perform on screen.

The answer assembled itself on the Sunset Strip.

What assembled there was not a spontaneous cultural eruption. It was a convergence of specific economic pressures, specific geographic conditions, and specific musicians. Ones who understood that the rules of visibility had changed and that the bands who adapted to those rules would inherit the commercial infrastructure that arena metal had built. Los Angeles in the early 1980s was the ideal environment for that convergence. The city had the Whisky a Go Go and the Roxy and the Troubadour — club venues with direct connections to the major label A&R infrastructure that could move a band from club draw to label interest to national exposure with a speed that no other city's infrastructure could match. It had a visual culture — the film industry, the fashion industry, the specific aesthetic of Sunset Strip nightlife. That made image literacy a baseline competency rather than an acquired skill. And it had a concentration of musicians who had come from across the country specifically because Los Angeles was where the commercial music industry lived. This meant the talent pool was deep and the competitive pressure to develop a viable commercial identity was constant and intense.

Mötley Crüe formed in 1981. Ratt's commercial breakthrough came in 1984. Poison relocated from Pennsylvania to Los Angeles in 1986 specifically because the infrastructure was there. Bon Jovi from New Jersey, operating within the same commercial logic from a different geographic base but feeding into the same label system and the same MTV pipeline. These bands did not emerge from a shared scene the way Birmingham had produced Sabbath and Priest, or the D.C. hardcore scene had produced Minor Threat and Fugazi. They emerged from a shared understanding of what commercial infrastructure required and a shared willingness to build music that met those requirements without apology.

That willingness is what the underground couldn't forgive and what the commercial mainstream couldn't resist.

What the commercial mainstream couldn't resist was the solution these bands represented to a problem the industry had been accumulating since punk fractured the arena rock consensus. The problem was legibility. Heavy music in the early 1980s had become too many things at one time. Overall, too fragmented, too ideologically varied, too sonically diverse for a major label marketing department to build a coherent commercial identity around. Thrash was too aggressive for casual consumption. Hardcore was too politically confrontational for advertiser comfort. The emerging death metal and grindcore forms were too sonically extreme for any mainstream delivery system to carry. The underground was generating genuine evolutionary vitality and genuine commercial uselessness at the same time. Two were related — the vitality came from the refusal of the commercial logic, which made the music commercially useless by design.

Hair metal solved the readability problem. It gave industry heavy music it could describe in a sentence. Photograph for a cover, reduce to a three-minute single. Rotate on MTV and sell to an audience that wanted the volume and the distortion and the physical scale of heavy music. All without the ideological commitment or the sonic extremity the underground had made inseparable from those qualities. It separated heaviness as sensation from heaviness as confrontation. It delivered the sensation through the most efficient commercial delivery system available.

This is not a critique. It is a structural description of what the mutation accomplished and why it accomplished it when it did. Mötley Crüe and Bon Jovi and Poison were not cynics who had calculated the commercial formula and built product to satisfy it. They were musicians who wanted the largest possible audience for music they genuinely loved. Who understood that the path to that audience ran through MTV and the major label pipeline rather than the tape trading network. The authenticity was real. The adaptation was also real. Both things were true— which is exactly what made the mutation viable rather than merely cynical.

Heavy music had a new center. It was loud, it was visual, it was engineered for broadcast scale, and it was coming out of a television set in a living room near you every hour of every day.

The underground noticed. And responded the only way it knew how — by going further in the opposite direction.

Two systems now running in parallel. Two gravitational fields pulling heavy music in opposite directions. The polarity that would define the form for the rest of the decade had been established, and neither system had any interest in resolving it.

The collision was already scheduled. Neither side knew the date.

ENGINEERING THE SOUND (1983-1991)

The sound that came out of the commercial heavy mainstream in the mid-1980s did not happen by accident. It was built. They did this deliberately, technically, expensively. In specific rooms by specific people who understood that the transition from underground volatility to broadcast-compatible heaviness required solving a precise engineering problem. How do you preserve the physical impact of heavy music — the amplification, the distortion, the guitar density, the drumming weight? All while making it translucent enough for FM radio, televisual enough for MTV, and emotionally accessible.

The answer required a room. And the room that mattered most was on Devonshire Street in North Hollywood.

Sound City Studios had been operating since 1969 in a converted vaudeville theater in the San Fernando Valley. An unglamorous by Los Angeles standards, deliberately removed from the Sunset Strip's visual economy, a working facility rather than a prestige address. What it had was a live tracking room with acoustic properties that engineers and producers had been trying to understand and reproduce for decades. The room had a natural reverb characteristic. A specific relationship between its dimensions, its concrete walls, its isolation from external noise, and the way sound reflected and decayed within it. That produced a drum sound of depth and physical presence. You could hear the room on the record. That was the point. The room was part of the instrument.

The console anchoring Sound City's engineering capability was a Neve 8078. A British-built analog mixing board installed in 1972 that represented the state of the art at the time of its installation. By the mid-1980s it was already becoming an artifact. The digital recording technology was advancing rapidly, and major studios were investing in the new formats. The Neve 8078's analog signal path had a specific characteristic that digital recording of that era couldn't replicate. It added harmonic content to the signal as it passed through the circuitry. Not distortion in the pejorative sense — coloration, a warmth and density in the low-midrange frequencies that made recorded instruments sound physically present rather than technically accurate. Drums recorded through the Neve 8078 in Sound City's live room didn't just sound loud. They sounded like they were in the room with you.

That combination of the room's natural acoustic properties and the console's analog coloration produced a drum sound that became the sonic signature of mainstream American rock in the mid-1980's. Gated reverb, the production technique that defined the decade's drum sound, worked in Sound City's room with a specificity that other facilities struggled to match. The gate — an electronic processor that cut the reverb tail at a precise point rather than letting it decay naturally. When combined with the room's inherent acoustic depth produced a drum sound that was enormous and controlled. The snare hit with the weight of the room behind it and then stopped, cleanly, before the next beat. Physically massive. Rhythmically precise. Exactly the combination that broadcast-compatible heaviness required.

Fleetwood Mac recorded Rumours there in 1976. Neil Young tracked multiple records in that room. Tom Petty. REO Speedwagon. The room's history before the hair metal era was not heavy music. It was the broader American rock tradition working in a facility with specific acoustic properties that nobody fully understood but everybody wanted access. What changed in the early 1980s was not the room. It was who was booking it and what they were trying to build with what it offered.

Bruce Fairbairn was the most significant producer to understand how to use Sound City and facilities like it for the specific requirements of broadcast-compatible heaviness. A Canadian producer and arranger who had developed his engineering sensibility working with Vancouver rock bands in the late 1970's. Fairbairn brought a precise understanding of how to balance the competing demands of the form. How to preserve the guitar density and amplification weight gave heavy music its physical identity while creating the mix clarity that FM radio and MTV required. How to build drum sounds that felt massive without overwhelming the vocal frequencies. How to layer guitar tracks in ways that created sonic depth without muddying the midrange where the ear most clearly perceives melodic information.

His work with Aerosmith on Permanent Vacation in 1987 and Pump in 1989 demonstrated the production philosophy at its most fully realized. Aerosmith in 1987 were a band returning from a decade of creative and personal collapse. The original lineup reassembled, sober, and working with a producer who understood that their commercial resurrection required a sound that honored their hard rock identity while meeting broadcast requirements that hadn't existed when the band was last commercially relevant in the mid-1970's. Permanent Vacation gave Aerosmith back their physicality. The guitar crunch, the rhythmic punch, the Steven Tyler vocal presence. All while delivering it through a production that FM radio could play in heavy rotation and MTV could broadcast without the signal degrading into murk. The drums were massive and controlled. The guitars were dense and clear. The vocals sat above the instrumentation with a presence the band's 1970's recordings, for all their raw energy, had never achieved.

The record went triple platinum. The production philosophy it represented became the template.

Fairbairn's production of Slippery When Wet in 1986 makes the argument more precise than any theoretical description could. The record sold over twelve million copies in the United States alone. A commercial performance that no heavy music record had previously achieved and that demonstrated exactly what broadcast-compatible heaviness could accomplish when the engineering was executed correctly. The guitars were distorted and physically present. Nobody listening to "You Give Love a Bad Name" or "Livin' on a Prayer" was in any doubt they were hearing a heavy record. The drum sound was enormous, the rhythm section locked and physical, the guitar tone carrying the density and crunch the genre's identity required. And all of it was delivered with mixed clarity that FM radio could play in heavy rotation. That MTV could broadcast without signal degradation. And that a cassette player in a car could reproduce without the low-end collapsing into mud.

That last detail matters more than it might appear. The cassette was the primary domestic playback format of the mid-1980's. Not vinyl, not CD, which was still establishing itself as a consumer format, but the same cassette technology the underground was using to distribute demos through tape trading networks. The difference was that the underground cassettes were carrying fourth-generation copies of four-track recordings made in rehearsal spaces. Fairbairn's production was engineered to survive the signal degradation of cassette playback without losing its impact. The production anticipated every delivery medium — FM radio, MTV, cassette, and the emerging CD format. It was built to perform in all of them. That multi-format engineering discipline was not something the underground had any reason to develop. It was specific to the commercial system, and it gave the commercial system a reach that the underground's infrastructure, for all its evolutionary vitality, could not match.

Fairbairn was not alone in developing this production philosophy. Tom Allom's work with Priest on Screaming for Vengeance in 1982 and Defenders of the Faith in 1984 had established an earlier version of the same discipline. Heavy guitar tones delivered with FM clarity; drum sounds massive enough for arena playback but controlled enough for radio. Mutt Lange's production of Pyromania in 1983 pushed the vocal layering and hook architecture further than anyone had previously attempted in a heavy context. Building chorus sections from dozens of stacked vocal tracks that created a sound intimate and enormous. Each producer was solving the same engineering problem from a slightly different angle. The collective result was a production language for heavy music that the commercial infrastructure could carry, and the underground had no interest in speaking.

Sound City's contribution extended beyond the records made within its walls. The facility functioned as proof of concept. A demonstration that the acoustic properties of a specific room, combined with the right console and the right engineering philosophy. Producing a heavy sound of sufficient clarity and physical presence to satisfy both the genre's identity requirements and the broadcast infrastructure's technical demands. The Neve 8078 became a reference point. Engineers who had worked there brought knowledge of what that console's analog signal path contributed to the sound into their work at other studios. The room's acoustic philosophy — the understanding that physical space was part of the instrument. That the relationship between the room's dimensions and the microphone placement with the console's signal processing was what produced the sound rather than any single element in isolation. It influenced how studios across Los Angeles and beyond were designed and operated throughout the decade.

What Sound City represented, structurally, was the industrialization of a specific approach. The underground's production aesthetic — raw, fast, honest about its resource limitations, prioritizing speed of capture over quality of reproduction — was not an aesthetic choice in isolation. It was an honest reflection of what the underground's infrastructure could afford. What the underground's values required. Sound City and the production philosophy it anchored represented the opposite end of the same spectrum. An approach that required significant capital investment, significant technical expertise, significant time in the studio, and a deliberate orientation toward the broadcast requirements. You could not make a Sound City record on a four-track in a rehearsal space. You could not make a tape trading demo in Sound City's live room. The two production philosophies were expressions of two incompatible infrastructural logics, and the music they produced sounded like what they were.

The engineering was not neutral. It was a declaration of intent. Every production decision Fairbairn and his peers made gated reverb snare, every layered guitar track, every vocal stack, every mix choice that prioritized clarity over density. A musical decision and an infrastructural alignment.

The sound said: we are making music for broadcast. We are making music for arenas. We are making music for the largest possible audience that the commercial delivery system can reach. We are not making music for a padded envelope moving through the postal system between people who find each other's addresses in the back pages of a photocopied zine.

Both systems were making the most of what their infrastructure offered. Both were producing music authentic to the logic of that infrastructure. And both by 1986 and 1987, producing music of sufficient quality and sufficient identity that the audience for each was growing rather than shrinking. The commercial mainstream expanding through MTV rotation and arena touring, the extreme underground expanding through the tape network and the escalation arms race the network sustained.

The polarity was not a sign of heavy music's fragmentation into irrelevance. It was a sign of heavy music's expansion into two simultaneous versions of itself. Each coherent, each vital, each running on a different fuel, and each heading toward a collision that the infrastructure of both systems had been designed to survive.

WAS IT REAL METAL? (1983-1991)

The question gets asked with the confidence of a verdict. Hair metal wasn't real metal. It was pop with distortion. It diluted the form. It betrayed the tradition. The underground knew it immediately and said so loudly, and that judgment has survived into the critical consensus that followed. The retrospective dismissal of the Sunset Strip era as a commercially cynical detour from heavy music's legitimate development. A phase the form had to pass through and recover from rather than a genuine mutation that deserves analytical attention on its own terms.

That verdict is wrong. Not morally wrong — there are no moral stakes in genre classification — but analytically wrong. This matters for a book whose argument depends on understanding what heavy music actually did and why it did it rather than what the underground decided it should have done instead. The verdict confuses two things that are genuinely distinct: structural heaviness and tonal mood. Conflating them produces the wrong conclusion about what hair metal was and what it accomplished. Separating them produces a more accurate account of how the mutation worked.

Structural heaviness is a specific set of sonic properties — high-gain amplification, distorted guitar tone, riff-centered composition, physical volume at the point of performance, the dominance of the low-midrange frequencies where the ear perceives weight and density. These properties are either present in a recording or they are not. They are measurable in the signal. They are audible in playback. They do not require interpretation.

Tonal mood is something different. It is the emotional register that the structural properties are used to generate. Whether the weight, the distortion, and the amplification are being deployed in the service of dread or celebration, confrontation or invitation, existential darkness, or aspirational fantasy.

Sabbath established the template for structural heaviness as the vehicle for tonal dread. The tuning, the tempo, the riff vocabulary, the lyrical register. All of it oriented toward a specific emotional experience that the underground had inherited and intensified with each successive mutation. The underground's escalation from Sabbath's dread through thrash's aggression through death metal's darkness through black metal's ideological hostility. A continuous intensification of the same tonal mood through increasingly extreme structural means. The mood and the structure had become so thoroughly identified with each other in the underground's aesthetic that the underground had stopped being able to distinguish between them. Dread felt like heaviness. Heaviness felt like dread. Separating the two felt like betrayal.

Hair metal separated them. Deliberately, structurally, and with complete awareness of what it was doing. Not in the sense that the musicians sat down and analyzed the distinction theoretically. In the sense that the music they made demonstrates the separation with unmistakable clarity. Mötley Crüe on Shout at the Devil in 1983 were playing through Marshall stacks at arena volume with guitar tones of genuine density and aggression. The amplification was real. The distortion was real. The physical impact on live performance volume was real. And the tonal mood was not dreadful. It was confrontational celebration. The specific register of a band that wanted you to feel the weight of the music as exhilaration rather than oppression. As an invitation to excess rather than a meditation on collapse.

That is not a lesser use for the structural properties. It is a different use of them. And difference is different from lesser, regardless of what the underground's aesthetic hierarchy insisted.

The structural properties that hair metal retained from the heavy music tradition are worth examining with precision. The critical dismissal of the form tends to obscure them under the weight of aesthetic objections. Start with amplification. The guitar tones on the significant hair metal records of the mid-1980's were produced through the same amplifier technology the underground was using. Marshall and Peavey stacks driven to the point of natural overdrive, the signal chain from guitar to amplifier to speaker cabinet generating the harmonic distortion that gives heavy music its characteristic sonic density. Eddie Van Halen's brown sound — the specific tone he developed through a modified Marshall Plexi and a homemade attenuator that allowed the amplifier to be driven at full power without the speaker volume becoming unmanageable in a studio environment. One of the most studied and imitated guitar tones of the decade precisely because it demonstrated what high-gain amplification could produce when approached with genuine sophistication. Van Halen's tone was not soft. It was not pop. It was a distorted guitar sound of genuine complexity and physical presence. The underground's own guitarists studied and learned from even as the underground's ideology required dismissing the context in which it appeared.

The riff remained central. Hair metal's compositional logic was riff-driven in the same fundamental sense as every previous phase of heavy music. The guitar figure anchoring the song, establishing its rhythmic and harmonic identity, prompting the listener's body to respond before the mind had processed the lyrical content. The riffs were simpler than thrash's technical escalations and less dissonant than the extreme underground's tonal experiments. Simplicity is not absence. A riff that is immediately memorable and physically impactful is doing exactly what a riff is supposed to do. The underground's escalating complexity had produced riffs of genuine sophistication that required repeated listening to fully absorb. Hair metal riffs were designed for immediate impact. Which is a different compositional priority operating within the same compositional framework.

The guitar solo survived. This matters because the solo had been one of punk's primary targets and had been deliberately suppressed in the hardcore tradition. A symbol of the hierarchical credentialism punk had rejected. Hair metal not only retained the guitar solo but elevated it. The solo as spectacle, as the moment in the song where technical mastery was put on explicit display for an audience trained to receive it. This purpose is for entertainment rather than intimidation. Randy Rhoads with Ozzy, Warren DeMartini with Ratt, George Lynch with Dokken. Guitarists of genuine technical capability whose solos demonstrated a command of the instrument. The underground's ideological rejection of virtuosity had specifically excluded solos from its own vocabulary. The underground had made a tactical decision to suppress technical display in service of access and confrontation. Hair metal made the opposite tactical decision. Both decisions were responses to specific pressures. Neither was inherently more authentic than the other.

The counterargument from the underground's position was not about structural properties. It was about what heaviness was for. And this is where the argument gets genuinely interesting rather than merely systematic.

The underground's position — stated explicitly in the hardcore and thrash traditions and implicitly in the extreme metal forms that followed. Heaviness was a weapon. A form of confrontation. A sonic enactment of the social, political and psychological pressures that the music's community was living under and refusing to accommodate. Sabbath's dread was a response to Birmingham's industrial collapse. Punk's aggression was a response to the class structure that arena rock had reproduced. Hardcore's speed was a response to Reagan's political cutback. Each phase of the underground's development had a specific external pressure that the music was responding to and that gave the music's extremity a social logic beyond mere aesthetic preference.

Hair metal's external pressure was different in kind. The Reagan era's consumer optimism — the specific ideological formation that combined economic deregulation with cultural conservatism and produced, in the entertainment industry, an enormous appetite for aspirational fantasy. Not the pressure of industrial collapse or political confrontation. It was the pressure of abundance, or at least the performance of abundance. The specific American cultural moment in which the appearance of prosperity was itself a political statement. The entertainment industry's job was to provide the fantasy infrastructure that made the appearance feel real. Hair metal was the heavy music of that moment. Not because the musicians were cynical operatives of the Reagan cultural project, but because they were human beings living in the same cultural moment as their audience. While making music that reflected what that moment felt like from the inside.

What it felt like, apparently, was loud, celebratory, excessive, and fun. Which are not less human experiences than dread and confrontation. They are different human experiences. And heavy music, it turned out, could serve both.

The alternative timelines reveal the structural logic of what actually happened by demonstrating what the alternatives would have required.

The first is the one the underground preferred and still prefers in retrospect. Thrash as the mainstream center. The argument runs that Metallica and Slayer and Megadeth were already achieving significant commercial traction by the mid-1980's. Thrash's aggression and technical sophistication represented a more honest development of heavy music's structural properties than hair metal's tonal reorientation. With sufficient label investment and production refinement thrash could have occupied the mainstream slot that hair metal filled. The argument is not implausible on its face. Master of Puppets sold respectably without significant radio or MTV support, which suggests the audience for aggressive, technically demanding heavy music was larger than the commercial infrastructure had assumed.

But the argument underestimates what MTV's visual economy requires. Thrash's visual identity — the denim and leather, aggressive physicality, the deliberate rejection of glamour and spectacle were not MTV-compatible. This is not a superficial objection. MTV's gatekeeping power operated through visual selection before sonic selection. A band had to be watchable before it could be listenable in MTV's programming logic. Watchable meant immediately legible in a three-minute video to an audience that was channel-surfing rather than actively seeking. Thrash's visual aesthetic communicated authenticity and aggression to an audience already inside the underground. To an audience outside it, the same visual aesthetic communicated opacity. A scene that knew what it was and wasn't particularly interested in explaining itself to you.

Hair metal's visual aesthetic was the opposite of opaque. The hair, the makeup, the leather and spandex, the deliberate theatricality. All of it communicated instantly and across demographic lines. You didn't need to know anything about heavy music's history to understand what Mötley Crüe looked like on a television screen. The image was its own explanation. That self-explanatory visual clarity was not accidental excess. It was the specific property that MTV's visual economy selected for, and it was the property that thrash, by design and by ideology, refused to develop.

The second alternative is more structurally interesting. The scenario in which the underground's tape trading infrastructure achieved distribution parity with the commercial system before MTV consolidated its gatekeeping power. If cheap duplication technology had arrived earlier, or if the postal exchange networks had reached sufficient density before the cable television infrastructure expanded, the extreme underground might have bypassed the commercial system entirely and established a parallel distribution model capable of reaching a mass audience without MTV mediation.

This alternative is fascinating precisely because it almost happened. Not in the 1980's but in the 1990's, when the internet began doing exactly what the tape trading network had been attempting to do at analog speed and postal cost. The digital distribution revolution the internet enabled after 2000 is the fulfillment of the logic the tape trading network had established in the 1980's. Music moving directly from producer to listener without commercial mediation. Scenes developing without geographic constraint. The gatekeeping function of the major label and the broadcast network becoming optional rather than mandatory. The underground was not wrong about where the distribution logic was heading. It was simply a decade and a half ahead of the technology that would make logic viable on a mass scale.

In 1985, capital still outweighed photocopiers. The tape trading network was reaching thousands of listeners simultaneously. MTV was reaching millions. The commercial infrastructure's advantage in scale was not a permanent condition of the music industry. It was a temporary consequence of the specific technological moment. The window between the naturalization of recording technology and the democratization of distribution technology. Production had become accessible, but distribution remained expensive. Hair metal filled that window. It was the mutation that the window selected for, and the window closed when the internet opened.

The third alternative — heavy music remaining permanently decentralized without a commercial center. The one that occurred, though not in the 1980's and not through the mechanism the underground had anticipated. After 1991, heavy music never re-centralized around a single dominant commercial form with the totality that hair metal had achieved. Grunge briefly occupied the mainstream slot but dissolved too quickly and was too internally contradictory to sustain the kind of commercial dominance hair metal had built over nearly a decade. The Black Album sold at hair metal scale but represented a specific band's commercial apex rather than a genre's consolidation. After that, the center held for shorter periods. Nu-metal's window, metalcore's window, each briefer and less total than the last. The fragmentation that the underground had been practicing since the mid-1980's became the permanent condition of the mainstream as well.

Hair metal was the last time heavy music had a unified commercial center. That is not a trivial achievement. It is the historical fact that the critical dismissal of the form consistently fails to reckon. The underground was right that hair metal altered the tonal mood. It was wrong that the alteration was a betrayal. It was an adaptation — the last successful adaptation to a centralized commercial infrastructure before that infrastructure became optional. What replaced it was not a better version of the same thing. What replaced it was the permanent fragmentation the underground had been building toward all along

THE THRONE BREAKS (1988-1992)

Every centralization generates its own demolition. This isn't pessimism — it is how systems built on escalation and distinction respond to consolidation. When a form stabilizes around a dominant center, the pressure that stabilization suppresses doesn't disappear. It builds at the margins, intensifying as the center grows stronger, until the margin generates enough force to displace it entirely. Birmingham displaced the blues-rock consensus. Punk displaced arena rock. Hardcore displaced punk. Each time the logic was the same. The center's success created the conditions for its own overthrow by making visible exactly what it had excluded to get there.

Hair metal's success was total enough to make its exclusions impossible to ignore.

By 1988 the commercial infrastructure hair metal had built operating at a scale heavy music had never seen. MTV rotation was generating national exposure for bands that two years earlier had been playing the Whisky a Go Go to three hundred people. Arena tours were filling venues that the previous generation had spent a decade building the audience to justify. Major label money was flowing into the Sunset Strip at a rate that made the DIY economics of the extreme underground look not just modest but irrelevant. The center was not just holding. It was expanding.

And the margins were watching. And the margins were responding.

The underground's response was not a coordinated campaign. It was automatic — every variable the commercial center had suppressed intensifying across scenes that had no direct contact with each other but were all responding to the same pressure from the same direction.

In Norway, the proto-black metal scene around Euronymous and Mayhem hardened its ideology in direct proportion to hair metal's visibility. The corpse paint that became black metal's visual signature was not developed in isolation from the commercial mainstream. It was developed in explicit opposition to it. Where hair metal's image communicated aspiration and accessibility, black metal's image communicated the opposite. The corpse paint was not beautiful. It was not aspirational. It was not designed to be legible to a channel-surfing audience in New Jersey. It was designed to repel that audience. To say in a single visual gesture that this music was not for them and had no interest in becoming so. The more polished the mainstream got, the uglier and more inaccessible black metal became in response.

The sonic philosophy followed the same logic. Euronymous's approach — deliberately degrades recording quality, embracing lo-fi murk as a principle rather than a limitation. A direct inversion of Fairbairn's. Where Fairbairn was engineering clarity, Euronymous was engineering opacity. Where Fairbairn built sounds that survived broadcast compression and FM radio, Euronymous built sounds that collapsed under those conditions and were better for collapsing. The degradation was the content. You couldn't play a Mayhem demo on MTV. That was the point.

Florida death metal was responding to the same pressure through different means. Where black metal's response was atmospheric and ideological, death metals was technical. The complexity Schuldiner was developing in Death's recordings through the late 1980's and early 1990's was complexity as resistance. A resistance to the simplification that commercial viability required. Hair metal's riffs were designed for immediate impact. You could sing them back after one listen. Death metal's riffs were designed for structural depth. You were still finding new things in them after fifty listens.

That opposition was structural before it was conscious. The Florida bands weren't primarily reacting to hair metal — they were following the internal logic of their own form. The competitive pressure of the tape trading network, the need to push further than the last demo. But the direction they were pushing was the exact opposite of where the mainstream was heading. When the center moves toward simplicity, the margins move toward complexity. When the center moves toward accessibility, the margins move toward exclusivity. The system generates opposition automatically because opposition is the only available distinction when the center has occupied all the accessible ground.

UK grindcore was at the furthest extreme of the same logic. Napalm Death's escalation of speed and brevity and abrasion was not separable from the cultural context. A mainstream producing music of increasing polish and uplift. The most radical gesture available was to produce music at the maximum possible distance from all three. The thirty-second song wasn't just a compositional choice. It was a statement about what music was for and who it was for. Hair metal said the audience should feel welcome. Grindcore said the audience should feel challenged to the point of exclusion. By 1989 the distance between those two positions was the largest it had ever been in the history of heavy music.

The schism went beyond aesthetic disagreement. The underground's hostility toward the commercial mainstream was active and energized. The kind that requires the object of its contempt to remain visible and dominant to sustain itself. The underground needed hair metal's dominance the way a resistance movement needs an occupation. Remove the commercial center and the underground's identity as its opponent becomes unnecessary. The contempt was a form of dependence.

Hair metal's relationship to the underground was more complicated. The commercial mainstream wasn't paying much attention to the extreme underground. The tape trading network was invisible to the commercial infrastructure. The extreme forms too marginal and too deliberately opaque to register as threats. But individual musicians within the mainstream were listening. The technical escalation of thrash, the rhythmic sophistication of the crossover scene, the production innovations the underground was discovering through resource constraint. All of it was feeding into the commercial mainstream's development in ways that were rarely acknowledged and are still rarely discussed.

Metallica is the most significant example of this. By the mid-1980's they had achieved a commercial scale that no other band operating within the underground's values had previously reached. Not through compromise but through the combination of underground credibility and mainstream accessibility that Master of Puppets demonstrated was possible. The record sold without radio support. Without MTV rotation. It sold because the audience for technically sophisticated, uncompromising heavy music was larger than the commercial infrastructure had assumed, and Metallica had found that audience through the same touring and word-of-mouth networks the underground had been using for a decade.

Metallica represented a third path. Not the commercial center's accessibility and not the underground's deliberate inaccessibility. A position that maintained the underground's sonic values while building toward commercial scale through the quality of the music rather than through production compromise. That path was narrow and specific to their combination of gifts and instincts. It wasn't a template other bands could follow. But its existence proved that the polarity between commercial mainstream and extreme underground was not the only available position.

The collapse came faster than anyone on either side had anticipated and from a direction neither system had been watching.

Seattle had been developing its own response to the same cultural pressures that had generated hair metal's dominance and the underground's escalation. Not in the deliberate ideological obscurity of black metal's anti-commercial posture. In the practical obscurity of a regional scene that hadn't yet connected to either the commercial mainstream or the underground's tape trading network with enough density to generate national visibility. The Pacific Northwest had Sub Pop Records, a small independent label with genuine aesthetic vision and minimal commercial reach. It had a cluster of bands — Mudhoney, Soundgarden, Alice in Chains, Nirvana. All creating through influences that combined the underground's sonic values with a melodic sensibility and an emotional register the extreme underground had specifically excluded.

The emotional register was the crucial variable. The extreme underground had built its identity around confrontation and abrasion. Hair metal had built its identity around celebration and spectacle. The Seattle scene was working in the register of damage. Depression, alienation, self-destruction — territory that neither sonic warfare nor aspirational fantasy had any interest in. This wasn't new ground for heavy music. Sabbath's dread had touched it. Joy Division had developed it with genuine sophistication. But the 1980's polarization between extremity and spectacle had abandoned it. The abandonment had left a sizable portion of the heavy music audience without a form that reflected what their lives felt like.

Nirvana found that audience. Not through strategy or calculation — through the accidental alignment of Cobain's artistic vision with the emotional needs of people the existing infrastructure hadn't been serving. Nevermind was recorded at Sound City in 1991. The same room, the same Neve 8078 that had anchored the commercial mainstream's most successful heavy records. Produced by Butch Vig with a clarity and physical presence the underground's lo-fi aesthetic had specifically rejected. The production was not underground. The label was DGC, a major. And the music demolished the commercial center the major label system had spent a decade building.

The demolition has been consistently misunderstood. The standard account treats Nevermind as authenticity defeating artifice. The real thing displacing the fake thing, the underground finally claiming the mainstream that had always been rightfully its territory. That account is satisfying as narrative and wrong as analysis.

Nevermind did not succeed because it was more authentic than the hair metal records it displaced. Authenticity is not a measurable property of recordings, and it is not what audiences respond to when they choose one form of music over another. Nevermind succeeded because it arrived at the precise moment when the commercial infrastructure sustaining hair metal was already destabilizing from within. MTV's programming logic was shifting. The major labels' investment in the Sunset Strip was generating diminishing returns. The audience hair metal had built was beginning to feel the fatigue that follows oversaturation. The moment when a form that has been everywhere for long enough starts to feel like furniture rather than music.

Hair metal had been everywhere for a decade. The visual

codification that had been its strength had become its vulnerability. When every band looks the same and every chorus resolves the same way and every solo occupies the same position in the same three-minute format, the form has exhausted its capacity for surprise. And music without surprise cannot hold an audience that came to heavy music precisely because it wanted to feel something unexpected and real.

Nevermind was surprising. Not because it was more extreme — it wasn't, by any sonic measure — but because it came from a direction the existing commercial logic hadn't prepared anyone to expect. The quiet verse and the loud chorus. The melodic accessibility on top of the guitar density. The emotional directness — not aspirational fantasy, not ideological confrontation, but something personal and damaged and honest about what it felt like to be alive in 1991. The audience recognized it immediately because they had been waiting for it without knowing they were waiting.

The commercial infrastructure responded fast. Within months of Nevermind's release in September 1991, every major label was signing bands from Seattle and everywhere that sounded like Seattle. The A&R infrastructure that had spent a decade on the Sunset Strip pivoted overnight — not because the industry had suddenly developed an appreciation for authenticity but because the sales figures showed the audience's preference had shifted and the industry's job was to follow. Pearl Jam. Soundgarden. Alice in Chains. Stone Temple Pilots. The commercial infrastructure absorbed the Seattle sound and reproduced it at scale with the same efficiency it had applied to hair metal a decade earlier.

And in doing so, it began exhausting the Seattle sound the same way it had exhausted the Sunset Strip sound. Oversaturation. Homogenization. A specific emotional register transformed into a genre with requirements and conventions and visual codification as rigid as anything hair metal had developed. By 1994 grunge was already becoming furniture. By 1996 it was an artifact.

What the throne's collapse revealed was not that the commercial center had been illegitimate. It had been entirely legitimate — genuine musical talent operating within the specific constraints of a specific infrastructure at a specific cultural moment. What it revealed was that the commercial center was in temporary condition, not a permanent one. And the infrastructure that had made possible the MTV gatekeeping function, the major label investment model, the arena touring circuit — was beginning to show the structural limitations the underground had always insisted it contained.

MTV shifted its programming logic in the early 1990's not out of aesthetic conscience but out of economic necessity. The advertising model required demographic freshness. It required the channel to be the place where new things happened rather than where established things were confirmed. Hair metal's saturation had made it the latter. Nevermind demonstrated the former was still available. The shift wasn't ideological. It was economic. The same logic that selected hair metal in 1983 selected grunge in 1991. Not because grunge was more deserving but because grunge was what the freshness requirement demanded at that moment.

The major label investment model cracked through the mechanism of the advance. Upfront payments against future royalty earnings that had to be recouped before the artist saw income. Advances calibrated to hair metal's commercial scale couldn't survive the post-Nevermind market. The recalibration produced a contraction that hit not just the Sunset Strip bands whose moment had passed but the entire major label infrastructure built around the assumption of hair metal's continued dominance.

The arena touring circuit proved the most durable. The economics of large venues didn't disappear when the dominant form changed. But the circuit's relationship with the mutation cycle changed. In the hair metal era, the arena tour was the endpoint of a clear commercial pipeline. MTV generated exposure, album sales generated revenue, the arena tour converted revenue into the largest possible audience at the highest possible price. After 1991, that pipeline fragmented. The bands filling arenas were increasingly the bands that had built their audience before the pipeline broke. Metallica, Aerosmith, the hair metal acts that had achieved enough scale to sustain touring without continued radio and MTV support — rather than the bands currently generating the most attention or investment.

The throne had broken. What replaced it was not a new throne. What replaced it was the permanent condition the underground had been building toward since 1977. Fragmentation as the default state, mutation as the continuous condition, no single form achieving enough dominance to define what heavy music was for long enough to exhaust itself and generate its own replacement. The cycle that had run from Birmingham through punk through hardcore through thrash through hair metal — each phase generating the conditions for its own displacement — had completed its last full rotation.

After 1992, the cycle didn't stop. It accelerated. But it never again produced a center stable enough to anchor the whole thing. The fragmentation became the principle. The mutation became the product. The audience heavy music had built across three decades was large enough and diverse enough to sustain all the competing sub-genres without any of them needing to dominate.

Heavy music had become too large to have a king. The throne hadn't just broken. It had become structurally unnecessary.

Chapter 7 has examined the last successful centralization of heavy music around a unified commercial identity — the convergence of MTV's visual economy, major label investment, Sound City's production philosophy, and the Sunset Strip's specific conditions that produced hair metal's decade of dominance. It has also examined the structural opposition that dominance generated in the extreme underground and the specific mechanism by which the dominance collapsed when Nirvana arrived from a direction neither system had been watching. Chapter 8 will examine what the Black Album was — not the commercial juggernaut the industry narrative built around it but the last object capable of commanding every distribution pipeline, and why nothing has managed to do the same.

CHAPTER EIGHT

When One Band Held the Crown

THE LAST THRONE (1991-1992)

The Black Album did not arrive as a surprise. It arrived as an inevitability that nobody had fully articulated until it existed.

By 1991 heavy music had spent a decade fragmenting along every available axis. The extreme underground was running on tape trading and competitive escalation with no commercial ceiling and no commercial interest. Hair metal had built a commercial empire on MTV rotation and arena touring and was starting to show the fatigue that follows a decade of oversaturation. Thrash had achieved genuine commercial traction without compromise and was now facing the contradiction that success always creates for forms built on refusal. What do you do when the audience you built by rejecting the mainstream becomes large enough to constitute a mainstream of its own? Grunge was assembling itself in Seattle in relative obscurity, working through influences and an emotional register that neither the commercial mainstream nor the extreme underground had much interest in.

Into that fragmented landscape Metallica released an album with a near-black cover. A faint snake coiled in the darkness, minimal logo, no photograph, no fantasy illustration, no neon typography. The visual language communicated before the music did — this is not competing for your attention; it is assuming it — and the assumption was correct.

The Black Album achieved something the polarized

landscape of 1991 had made structurally improbable. It satisfied every distribution pipeline without compromising its identity for any of them. FM radio could play "Enter Sandman" in heavy rotation because the song's mid-tempo groove and hook architecture met the format's requirements without the tonal aggression that had kept thrash off radio throughout the previous decade. MTV could rotate the video because the band's visual presentation — black clothing, controlled lighting, performance-focused — gave the channel what its programming required without the glam coding the audience was already rejecting. Arena promoters could book the Wherever We May Roam tour with confidence because Metallica had spent a decade building the audience infrastructure that justified the booking. Not through a single commercial breakthrough but through relentless touring on every scale. And the metal audience — the underground-adjacent core that had been with the band since Kill 'Em All — could accept the record's commercial success without the credibility collapse that mainstream crossings had produced for every previous heavy act. The record sounded like Metallica. Heavier in the mix than ...And Justice for All, if not in the arrangement. More physically present. More authoritative. Not a compromise — a consolidation.

That convergence of every distribution pipeline around a single artifact is the structural definition of a commercial throne. It is not about artistic quality alone, though quality is a precondition. Plenty of high-quality records never achieve convergence because convergence requires specific alignment between the artifact's properties. Radio requires one thing. MTV requires another. The arena circuit requires a third. The subcultural audience requires a fourth. These systems are not designed to select the same properties. When a single record satisfies all of them at once it is because the record has navigated a specific set of structural conditions that exist only briefly, at specific cultural moments, before the systems' requirements diverge again.

The conditions that made the merger possible had been assembling for three years before the record's release. Hair metal's oversaturation had opened a gap at the commercial center. The mainstream heavy audience was ready for something that retained the form's physical identity without the visual codification that familiarity had made invisible. The extreme underground's escalation had created a reference point against which the Black Album's controlled heaviness registered as disciplined rather than commercial. It was possible to hear "Sad But True" as a heavy record in 1991 in a way that might not have been possible in 1986. And Metallica's specific position — a decade of underground credibility, significant but not mainstream-scale commercial success. A reputation for musical seriousness that no commercial ambition had compromised. The band arrived at the mainstream crossing with authority the mainstream couldn't dismiss and the underground couldn't deny.

Bob Rock's production was the mechanism that made the convergence audible. Rock had produced Mötley Crüe's Dr. Feelgood in 1989. The commercial heavy sound at its most fully realized and brought to the Black Album a production discipline that understood both the commercial mainstream's technical requirements and the extreme underground's physical standards. The low-end extension he achieved in the mix. The kick drum forward and isolated, the bass guitar audible and present in a way that ...And Justice for All's notorious bass-absent mix had specifically denied. This gave the record a physical weight the commercial mainstream's production had rarely prioritized. The guitars were dense enough to carry the harmonic information that heavy music requires. Clean enough that each riff's individual notes registered with precision. The drum sound was enormous without being murky, the snare crack clean in a way that translated across FM radio, MTV broadcast, and arena PAs.

The tempo was the most consequential production decision. ...And Justice for All had been inside the thrash arms race — songs long, picking relentless, tempo pushing toward the upper range of what the form had established as the standard for seriousness. The Black Album moderated the tempo deliberately, and the moderation was not a concession to accessibility. It was recognition that at arena scale, tempo and impact have an inverse relationship. That the underground's club-optimized aesthetic had no reason to have discovered. In a 20,000-seat venue, high-BPM thrash collapses at distance. The individual riff notes blur into a wall of the same mass that the ear cannot analyze from the back of the room. Mid-tempo riffs with space between the strikes land differently. The silence between the downbeats allows the low-end of each strike to bloom through the PA before the next strike arrives. Bloom is what the body feels rather than the ear hears. "Sad But True" at arena volume was not the controlled aggression of thrash's velocity. It was something slower and heavier and more total. A riff that didn't move past you but settled on you, that the body had no mechanism for ignoring.

That physical authority at scale was the Black Album's defining property and the property that made it the last throne rather than merely the largest commercial success of its moment. Every previous commercial throne in heavy music had required some form of supplement. Arena rock's theatrical distance, hair metal's visual spectacle, the costuming that all of them had used to amplify the music's physical impact. The Black Album required none of that. It was heavy enough, on its own terms, to command attention at the scale the commercial infrastructure required. It achieved that weight through consolidation of force rather than external amplification.

The throne it built was the last one. Not because no subsequent heavy record achieved significant commercial success. Because no subsequent heavy record achieved the specific convergence of every distribution pipeline around a single artifact with unified legitimacy across both the mainstream and the subcultural audience. The systems had been diverging since 1991. By the mid-1990's the divergence was permanent. Radio formats had splintered. MTV's programming logic had shifted and fragmented further. The arena circuit had decoupled from the album cycle. The subcultural audience had divided along the fault lines the extreme underground's arms race had been deepening since the mid-1980's.

A stronger claimant did not overthrow the throne. It became structurally impossible to rebuild. The conditions that had made the convergence possible dissolved and they dissolved permanently. Every subsequent attempt at heavy music's commercial centralization — grunge's brief occupation of the mainstream slot, nu-metal's broader but shallower penetration, metalcore's more recent commercial moment — achieved some subset of the convergence without achieving all of it. The subset they achieved was always smaller than what the Black Album had unified.

Heavy music was too large to have a king. The throne hadn't just broken. It had become structurally redundant.

THE AUSTERITY WEAPON (1991-1992)

The production philosophy Bob Rock brought to the Black Album was not a refinement of what Fairbairn had built at Sound City. It was a structural inversion — a deliberate dismantling of the production logic that had defined broadcast-compatible heaviness for the previous decade, executed with enough precision that the dismantling sounded like an arrival rather than a departure.

Fairbairn's philosophy had been additive. Layer the guitars. Stack the vocals. Build the chorus until the accumulated mass of the arrangement created the emotional impact rather than any single element within it. Slippery When Wet and Permanent Vacation were achievements of accumulation. Their power came from the density of what had been added to the signal rather than from the clarity of what remained when everything unnecessary had been stripped away. That additive logic was the commercial standard throughout the mid-to-late 1980's. It worked. FM radio rewarded layered vocal harmony. MTV rewarded sonic fullness. The cassette format's limited dynamic range was less damaging to dense mixes than to sparse ones.

By 1991 the additive logic had exhausted itself. Not because the techniques had stopped working — they hadn't. The cultural context had changed. Density had become the default. Every significant commercial heavy record of the previous five years had been dense. The ear had adapted the way it adapts to any repeated stimulus. What had been foreground had become furniture. The additive logic had produced its own invisibility.

Rock understood this and built the Black Album around its opposite. The philosophy was subtractive — identify the essential elements, reinforcing them to maximum impact, and removing everything competing with them for the listener's attention. The guitars were present but not overlayered. Two tracks rather than the four or six commercial standards had established. The reduction creating midrange clarity where the riff's individual notes lived that dense layering had obscured. Hetfield's vocals were clean and present without the harmonic stacking hair metal had used to broaden appeal. All delivered without supplementary layers that would have softened his authority and reduced it from command to invitation. The arrangements were stripped to their structural core. Fewer riffs per song. More repetition of the riffs that remained. The reduction created space for the rhythm section's physical impact to register in a way that complex arrangements had always prevented.

The kick drum was the most consequential single element in the production. In the dense commercial mixes of the hair metal era, the kick had been present but not prominent. One element among many, its low-end contribution audibles but not foregrounded. Absorbed into the arrangement's general heaviness. Rock isolated it. Brought it forward in the mix. Gave it low-end extension the album's overall frequency balance could support. Locked it to the palm-muted downstrokes of the rhythm guitar with a precision that made the rhythmic relationship between the two instruments feel like a single event rather than two parallel ones. The result was a rhythmic impact the body registered before the ear processed it. A physical phenomenon rather than a sonic one. The low-end of the kick and the guitar arrived and with a force that dense mixes had never achieved. Dense mixes had never prioritized the clarity that made the impact possible.

The Black Album cover communicated the production philosophy before anyone heard a note. A near-black field. A faint snake coiled in the darkness, barely visible. The Metallica logo in matte black against the glossy black background, readable only at the right angle in the right light. No photograph. No fantasy illustration. No color. No information beyond the minimum necessary to identify the artifact.

In the visual economy of 1991, that cover was an act of aggression. MTV's visual arms race had been running for a decade. Each cycle requires higher production values, more elaborate costuming, more saturated color, more visual information per second to compete for the attention of an audience trained to require escalating stimulation to register anything as significant. The Black Album cover refused the competition entirely. It did not attempt to win. It removed itself from the race and forced the attention economy to come to it. An object that refuses to compete for attention in the field of competing objects becomes the most attention-commanding object in the field. Austerity becomes contrast. Silence becomes the loudest signal.

The stage presentation mirrored the cover with the same logic. Black clothing on a dark stage. Controlled lighting that illuminated the performance without adding theater. No costume elements. No visual narrative. No choreography asking the audience to watch rather than feel. The Wherever We May Roam tour presented Metallica as a sound-delivery system with a human interface. The visual presentation stripped to the minimum necessary to sustain the audience's physical presence in the arena while directing all available attention toward the sonic event. This was not anti-spectacle as ideology. It was anti-spectacle as engineering. The recognition that every element of visual spectacle competed with the music for the audience's attention, and that the music's physical authority was sufficient to command that attention without competition if the competition was removed.

The contrast with grunge's concurrent visual philosophy reveals the Black Album's specific structural position. Grunge had developed its own form of visual subtraction — the flannel, the deliberate anti-fashion, the visible discomfort with the machinery of stardom. But grunge's subtraction was full of meaning. The flannel said something about authenticity and class and the rejection of aspiration. The slouched posture said something about alienation and doubt. The specific discomfort of finding yourself famous for music you made in basements. Grunge's visual austerity was dense with information. It required interpretation. It positioned the band within a cultural conversation about authenticity and commerce.

Metallica's visual austerity communicated nothing beyond presence. The black clothing didn't make a statement about authenticity. The minimal stage design didn't signal indecision about commercial success. The absence of theatrical elements didn't position the band within any cultural discourse. It simply directed attention toward the sound. Not meaningful silence — functional silence. A delivery system that had eliminated everything not required for delivery.

That functional silence was the austerity weapon's most significant achievement and the property that most completely explains the Black Album's cross-demographic reach. A record whose visual presentation required interpretation could be positioned. When placed within a cultural discourse, associated with a community, made to stand for something beyond music. Grunge stood for something. Hair metal had stood for something. The underground's various forms stood for something, often at considerable ideological length. The Black Album stood for heaviness. Nothing more specific than that. And heaviness, stripped of its ideological supplements and its tonal qualifications and its subcultural memberships. Something a significantly larger audience could access than any of the more positioned forms could reach.

Austerity was not a limitation. It was the mechanism of the reach.

THE CEILING BUILT (1992-1996)

Every consolidation generates the pressure that breaks it. The Black Album's achievement was total enough that the pressure it generated was proportionally total. Not a single challenge from a single direction but a fracturing along every axis the compressed.

The fracturing was structural rather than reactive. The musicians who responded to the Black Album's commercial dominance were not, for the most part, sitting in rehearsal rooms saying we need to sound like the opposite of Metallica. They were following the internal logic of their own forms. But the direction those internal logics pointed was the opposite direction from the Black Album's controlled authority. When a center achieves sufficient mass, the margins don't just move away from it. They accelerate away from it. The center's gravitational pull and the margin's centered force are the same phenomenon experienced from various positions.

Pantera was the most significant and most direct response to the Black Album's specific achievement. Formed in Arlington, Texas in the early 1980's as a glam band —

genuinely, unironically, with the hair and the image and the Sunset Strip ambitions intact. Pantera had spent the late 1980's developing a musical identity that progressively stripped the glam elements. They replaced them with rhythmic aggression that had no precedent in either the commercial mainstream or the extreme underground. Cowboys from Hell in 1990 announced the transformation. Vulgar Display of Power in 1992 completed it.

The specific properties of Vulgar Display of Power in relation to the Black Album reveal the structural logic of the fracturing with unusual clarity. Pantera was responding to the same question Metallica had answered. How do you make heavy music that commands attention at scale without spectacle and without the speed escalation that the underground's arms race had made the standard measure of seriousness? Where the Black Album answered with controlled authority — the mid-tempo groove, the disciplined repetition, the low-end that settled on the audience rather than moving past them. Pantera answered with volatile authority. The same rejection of spectacle. The same rejection of speed for its own sake. But where Metallica's authority was architectural — weight distributed evenly across the arrangement — Pantera's authority was percussive. Dimebag Darrell's guitar tone carried an abrasiveness the Black Album's production had specifically engineered away. Phil Anselmo's vocal delivery operated in a register of genuine aggression that Hetfield's controlled authority had no interest in. Vinnie Paul's drumming brought rhythmic violence to the groove metal framework that the Black Album's precision had deliberately excluded.

The distinction matters because it demonstrates that the Black Album's answer was not the only available answer. It was one answer, determined by Metallica's specific musical identity and Bob Rock's specific production philosophy and the specific cultural moment of 1991. Pantera's answer was equally valid and structurally opposite. Vulgar Display of Power eventually sold over nine million copies worldwide. Demonstrating that the audience for heavy music at scale was not a single audience with a single preference but a field of audiences with overlapping but distinct requirements that different forms could satisfy in different ways.

The extreme underground's response operated on a different axis entirely. Where Pantera recalibrated the weight and variables within the commercial framework, the extreme underground responded by intensifying the variables the Black Album had specifically suppressed. Complexity, dissonance, tonal darkness, production rawness, ideological extremity. The Norwegian black metal scene's consolidation in 1992 and 1993 around the aesthetic Euronymous had been developing. The corpse paint, the lo-fi production ideology, the anti-commercial philosophical framework that Varg Vikernes and Burzum were developing and with more violence. Not primarily a response to Metallica. But the timing and intensity of the consolidation were shaped by the cultural context the Black Album had established. When the commercial center achieves maximum polish and maximum controlled authority, the maximum available contrast is maximum rawness and maximum hostility. Black metal's specific aesthetic choices were not random. They were the furthest available distance from the Black Album's specific aesthetic choices, and the distance was the point.

Death metal's technical escalation in the same period followed the same oppositional logic through different means. Schuldiner's development of Death's musical vocabulary through Human in 1991 and Individual Thought Patterns in 1993 moved in the exact opposite direction from the Black Album's subtractive philosophy. By adding compositional complexity, adding rhythmic sophistication, adding harmonic language the extreme metal tradition had not previously explored. The building arrangements of genuine musical depth that rewarded sustained critical attention. The opposition was not conscious of antagonism. It was the automatic response of a form built on escalation and distinction to a center that had achieved its dominance through simplification and consolidation.

Alternative metal occupied the most complex position in relation to the Black Album because it was working in the commercial space the Black Album had defined. Refusing the specific aesthetic framework that had defined it. Tool's Undertow in 1993 and Soundgarden at their most developed were building heavy music of genuine ambition in the commercial space. Major label releases, MTV presence, arena-scale touring while pushing against the rhythmic, textural, and compositional boundaries. The Black Album's controlled authority had established as the commercial standard. Tool's specific contribution was the reintroduction of complexity density into the commercial framework. Long songs with non-standard time signatures and arrangements that developed through sustained internal logic rather than verse-chorus repetition. The songs demanded something from the listener beyond physical response. They required sustained attention and rewarded it with a depth of musical experience the Black Album's immediate authority had specifically traded away.

The groove metal response — Pantera's specific mutation spreading through bands like White Zombie, whose La Sexorcisto: Devil Music, Vol. 1 arrived in 1992, and the broader Texan and Southern metal infrastructure Pantera had seeded — represented the most commercially significant fracture point because it operated closest to the Black Album's own territory. These bands were not trying to out-Metallica Metallica. They were finding the available space adjacent to the throne.

What all these responses had in common was that none of them achieved the Black Album's specific convergence. The simultaneous satisfaction of every distribution pipeline with unified legitimacy across both the mainstream and the subcultural audience. Pantera came closest, building genuine commercial scale and genuine subcultural credibility. The roughness that was the source of their authority also limited their FM radio reach and MTV rotation in ways the Black Album's controlled authority had not been limited. Tool built a commercial presence of genuine scale and a critical reputation of genuine significance. They sacrificed the immediate ease of access that cross-demographic reach required. The extreme underground's various forms built subcultural legitimacy of the highest order and commercial scale of the most modest kind.

The throne had become a ceiling. And the ceiling was visible to every form of heavy music. The specific altitude the Black Album had achieved, the specific set of properties that had made the achievement possible, and the specific ways those properties constrained the available space for development. You could move toward the ceiling from below or move away from it toward the margins. You could not exceed it because the conditions that had made it possible had dissolved with the cultural moment that had produced it.

After 1993 the center of heavy music's commercial landscape was not occupied by a single dominant form. It was occupied by a field of competing forms. Each with its own audience. Each with its own distribution infrastructure. Each with its own relationship to the commercial mainstream's requirements. None of them achieved the convergence the Black Album had, all of them operating in the space the convergence had defined and then vacated.

The fragmentation was not a failure. It was the form's natural condition. The condition the underground had been building toward since Birmingham, the condition that every centralization had temporarily suppressed and every collapse had restored. The Black Album had been the last suppression. What followed was not the restoration of a previous condition but the establishment of a new one.

Heavy music after 1993 did not have a center. It had a history. The thirty-year accumulation of mutations and displacements that this book has traced from Birmingham to the Sunset Strip to the tape trading networks to the Black Album's last throne. And it had a future. The competing kingdoms that the throne's dissolution had made permanent, each running on its own logic, each feeding its own escalation, each finding its own audience in the permanently fragmented landscape that the underground had always been building and the commercial mainstream had always been temporarily interrupting.

The interruptions were over. The underground's logic had won. Not by defeating the commercial mainstream but by outlasting it. By building an infrastructure and an audience and a set of values that survived every centralization and every collapse by the commercial system to define what heavy music was and who it was for.

Heavy music after the Black Album did not need a king. It needed what it had always needed — the next mutation, the next escalation, the next sound that nobody had heard before reaching the next room where someone was waiting for it without knowing they were waiting.

The ceiling it built was the last ceiling. After this, there were only floors — and every floor was someone else's ceiling.

Chapter 8 examined the Black Album as the last centralized heavy object — the final moment when a single artifact commanded every distribution pipeline simultaneously with unified legitimacy across both the mainstream and the subcultural audience. The three sub-chapters have traced the specific mechanisms of that achievement — the rhythmic authority that replaced speed escalation, the austerity weapon that replaced spectacle, and the ceiling that the consolidation built and the fractures that the ceiling generated. Chapter 9 will examine what happened when the center dissolved permanently — the specific forms that emerged from the rubble of the last throne to define heavy music's permanent fragmentation through the final decade of the century.

CHAPTER NINE
When Nothing Could Centralize

HOSTILE AUTHORITY (1992-1996)

The Black Album had solved a specific problem so completely that the solution itself became the next problem. Metallica had demonstrated that heaviness could command global scale through controlled authority. Mid-tempo precision, low-end consolidation, the subtractive production philosophy that gave each element maximum impact by removing everything competing with it. The demonstration was total. The commercial dominance was total. And total demonstrations of any principle in heavy music have always generated the same response. The immediate search for what the demonstration excluded.

What the Black Album was not – was volatile. The authority it commanded was architectural — stable, controlled, load bearing in the structural sense that the riffs were designed to sustain weight rather than generate friction. "Sad But True" didn't threaten you. It settled on you. The distinction matters because heavy music's identity had been built on threat as much as weight. The confrontational directness that ran from Sabbath's dread through punk's aggression through hardcore's speed through thrash's precision was always partly about the relationship between the music and the audience being adversarial rather than communal. The Black Album had resolved that adversarial relationship into something more like command. The audience didn't need to be threatened. It needed to be controlled. And control at arena scale required the kind of stable authority that threat tends to undermine.

Pantera understood this and built their entire post-glam identity around its opposite.

The transformation Pantera executed between their glam-era recordings and Cowboys from Hell in 1990 is one of the most complete musical reinventions in the history of heavy music. Not a gradual evolution but a structural break. The band shedding an entire aesthetic vocabulary and replaced it with something that had no direct precedent in either the commercial mainstream or the extreme underground. The glam elements disappeared entirely. What replaced them was a rhythmic philosophy that Dimebag and Vinnie Paul had been developing in the rehearsal rooms of Arlington, Texas. A specific conviction that suggested they had been working toward it long before the commercial context made it legible.

Vulgar Display of Power in 1992 is the document that makes philosophy fully audible. The record arrived twelve months after the Black Album and the association was immediate. Two heavy records of significant commercial ambition, both rejecting spectacle, both operating in the mid-to-slow tempo range the Black Album had established as the new standard for serious heavy music. Both prioritize physical impact over technical escalation.

Where the Black Album's riffs repeated like law — symmetrical, load bearing, arriving on the downbeat with the predictable authority of a structure that knows it doesn't need to surprise you because it is simply too large to avoid. Pantera's riffs lurched and struck with a rhythmic irregularity that made every arrival feel like a threat rather than a confirmation. The stressed chugging patterns Dimebag developed- The palm-muted figures that broke symmetrical phrasing and landed on beats the ear hadn't predicted. This created a specific kind of tension the Black Album had specifically engineered away. The silence between the Black Album's strikes was atmosphere. The silence between Pantera's strikes was anticipation of impact. The held breath before something arrives that you know is going to hurt.

Anselmo's vocal delivery operated in a register Hetfield's controlled authority had no interest in approaching. Where Hetfield commanded, Anselmo confronted — the delivery not the assertion of a position of strength but the aggression of someone who wanted the confrontation for its own sake. Who found the threatening of the audience not a means to an end but the end itself. The specific anger of Vulgar Display of Power and Far Beyond Driven in 1994 was not the mythologized dread of the early Sabbath tradition or the political confrontation of the hardcore tradition. It was something more personal and more volatile. The anger of people who had something specific to prove and were proving it at volume.

The production reflected the philosophy with the same structural logic that Bob Rock's production had reflected Metallica's. Terry Date's work on Vulgar Display of Power was cleaner than the extreme underground's lo-fi standard but significantly rawer than the Black Album's controlled clarity. The guitar tone was sharper and drier — less low-end bloom, more midrange abrasion, and the frequency profile optimized for friction rather than mass. The drum sound was forward and aggressive rather than architectural. Vinnie Paul's snare hitting with a crack that felt combative rather than authoritative. The kit's overall presentation suggesting a drummer who was attacking the instrument rather than playing it.

The commercial result confirmed that the Black Album's specific solution was not the only available one. Vulgar Display of Power eventually sold over nine million copies worldwide. Far Beyond Driven debuted at number one on the Billboard 200 in 1994. A commercial achievement that demonstrated Pantera had built an audience of genuine scale without the radio accessibility or the MTV rotation dominance that the Black Album's production had been engineered to achieve. The audience found Pantera through the touring circuit and word-of-mouth networks. The same infrastructure the underground had always relied on. The commercial scale was built on underground foundations rather than commercial pipelines.

That infrastructure distinction is what separated groove metal's commercial success from the Black Album's structural supremacy. Pantera achieved commercial scale. They did not achieve pipeline convergence. FM radio could not play Vulgar Display of Power in heavy rotation because the record's abrasiveness exceeded the format's tolerance for confrontation. MTV rotated Pantera's videos but without the frequency the Black Album's visual austerity had generated. The visual presentation was sufficiently aggressive to complicate the channel's advertiser relationships in ways that Metallica's black-on-black minimalism had specifically avoided. The subcultural legitimacy was genuine and intact. The extreme underground respected Pantera in a way it had not respected hair metal. The legitimacy was specific to the metal and hardcore communities rather than universal across heavy music's various factions.

What Pantera proved was structural and consequential regardless of the pipeline limitations. They proved that the Black Album's controlled authority was not the final form of post-spectacle heaviness. The rejection of glam's visual economy and thrash's speed escalation did not require Metallica's specific aesthetic solution. The available space between the commercial mainstream's requirements and the extreme underground's deliberate detachment was larger and more varied than the Black Album's single occupancy had suggested. Groove metal filled a portion of that space with a form of heaviness that retained commercial ambition without commercial compromise. The music's own terms rather than through the production and tonal adjustments that meeting the commercial infrastructure's requirements had always previously demanded.

Weight had gotten its teeth back. The center had not recovered them. And the distinction between those two facts would define the shape of heavy music's development for the rest of the decade.

THE FORTRESS & THE LABORATORY (1991-1998)

While Pantera was recalibrating the weight variables within reach of the commercial framework, two other responses to the Black Album's consolidation were developing in the opposite direction entirely. Not recalibrations of the center's specific properties but structural departures from the center's logic. Forms of heavy music that defined themselves by their distance from the commercial mainstream rather than by their proximity to it.

The distance was the point. And the two forms that built their identities around that distance did so through completely opposite methods. One stripping everything away until only ideology and atmosphere remained. One adding everything until only precision and complexity remained. Black metal built a fortress. Death metal built a laboratory. Both were responses to the same pressure. Neither was interested in the throne.

Norwegian black metal's consolidation in the early 1990's around the aesthetic Euronymous had been developing at his record store Helvete in Oslo. This was not primarily a musical development. It was an ideological one. A decision made explicitly and with considerable violence in some cases. The commercial mainstream's definition of heavy music was not just aesthetically insufficient but philosophically contaminating. That the appropriate response was not to compete with it on its own terms but to build a parallel world so thoroughly insulated from its values that contamination became structurally impossible.

The music this ideology produced was the most extreme available inversion of the Black Album's specific properties. Where Rock had engineered clarity, the black metal production philosophy engineered opacity. The Burzum and early Darkthrone recordings carrying a lo-fi murk so complete that instruments bled into each other within the riffs and became suggestions rather than definitions. The recording quality degraded to the point where the music sounded like it was being heard through a wall rather than through a speaker. This was not resource limitation. Euronymous and his circle had access to better recording technology than they used. The degradation was a choice. The same kind of choice as the production philosophy was inverting, but in the opposite direction and for opposite reasons. Where Fairbairn and Rock had engineered sounds that survived every broadcast compression and format translation intact, black metal engineered sounds that collapsed under those conditions and were better for the collapsing. A Darkthrone recording played on FM radio would have sounded like equipment failure. That was the point.

The visual ideology followed the same inversion logic. Corpse paint is the black metal visual signature that gets discussed most frequently as shock theater, as adolescent transgression, as the kind of extreme imagery that any committed countercultural movement eventually develops. That reading misses the structural function. Corpse paint in the early 1990's Norwegian context was not shock theater. It was a visual declaration of species difference. The deliberate construction of an appearance so thoroughly outside the conventions of human social presentation that it communicated. In a single visual register, the people wearing it had opted out of the social contract that human appearance normally signals membership. Hair metal's image had been aspirational — look at us, want to be us. Black metal's image was repellent by design — we are not for you, and we have no interest in becoming so and the distance between your world and ours is the entire point.

The music's atmosphere was the sonic equivalent of the corpse paint's visual function. Where the Black Album's controlled repetition had created the atmosphere of disciplined authority — a massive and stable force the audience could orient itself in relation. Black metal's tremolo-picked guitar sheets and blast-beat drumming and shrieked vocals created an atmosphere of cold hostility. You could not find a groove in a Mayhem recording because groove implied a relationship between the music and the body that black metal's aesthetic philosophy refused. The music wasn't for dancing and wasn't for the pit and wasn't for the communal physical experience that every previous form of heavy music had offered as its primary social function. It was for immersion in an atmosphere of absolute darkness. A solitary experience of sonic totality that the commercial infrastructure had no mechanism for delivering and no interest in developing.

Varg Vikernes of Burzum pushed the ideology to its logical and then its criminal extreme. The church burnings, the murder of Euronymous in 1993, the prison sentence that followed. In doing so both defined black metal's specific notoriety and complicated the scene's subsequent development in ways still being worked through. The violence was not incidental to the ideology. It was the ideology taken seriously, the anti-social philosophical framework enacted rather than performed. Whether that enactment was the scene's authentic expression or its pathological deformation is a question the scene itself has never fully resolved and cannot. The violence is too embedded in the early 1990's Norwegian scene's foundation to be cleanly separated from the music. Music is too significant to be reducible to violence.

What matters is that the black metal scene's consolidation established a template for heavy music's relationship to the commercial mainstream. Not the underground's traditional posture of operating outside the commercial system while hoping eventually to connect with a mass audience. A deliberate and total rejection of the mass audience as a category. A decision that the music's value was inversely proportional to its accessibility. That template proved durable and influential far beyond the Norwegian scene's specific geographic and ideological context. The fortress had been built. Subsequent heavy music scenes would choose whether to occupy it, extend it, or demolish it. The option was now permanently available in a way it had not been before Euronymous and Darkthrone and Burzum had defined its architecture.

Death metal's response to the post Black Album landscape was the laboratory's response to the same problem. How does heaviness maintain its identity and evolutionary vitality when the commercial center has achieved sufficient stability to define the form's mainstream parameters? Where black metal solved it by rejecting the parameters entirely, death metal solved it by developing musical properties so far beyond the commercial mainstream's capacity to absorb that the parameters became irrelevant through complexity rather than rejection.

Schuldiner's development of Death's musical vocabulary through the early and mid-1990's is the clearest single document of this process. The process was occurring across the Florida death metal scene and its international extensions at once. Human in 1991, Individual Thought Patterns in 1993, Symbolic in 1995, The Sound of Perseverance in 1998 — each record adding compositional sophistication, harmonic language, and rhythmic complexity that pushed the death metal framework further from anything. Pushing it toward a musical depth the commercial infrastructure had never been capable of generating. Schuldiner was not trying to make inaccessible music. He was trying to make complete music. Music that honored the full range of his musical ideas without constraining those ideas to fit any external requirement, commercial or subcultural. Inaccessibility was a byproduct rather than a goal, which is what makes Death's development analytically different from black metal's deliberate construction of inaccessibility as the primary aesthetic principle.

The technical properties death metal was developing in this period including lower tunings anchoring the tonal mass, the hyper-precise palm-muted riff layering creating rhythmic density. It did it without sacrificing individual note clarity, complex time signatures, and rhythmic displacements. Making the music's internal logic demanding rather than immediately legible. The clinical double-bass drumming operates as a rhythmic machine rather than a musical personality. Not properties the commercial mainstream could absorb and reproduce at scale. They required too much from the listener and too much from the musicians. The investment of attention and technical capability that death metal demanded was precisely the investment the commercial infrastructure's economics had always required the music to minimize. The commercial system's fundamental logic being that the audience's investment should be as small as possible to maximize the potential audience size.

Death metal's laboratory had been running that logic in reverse since the mid-1980's. The post-Black Album period was when the reversal became most complete and most productive. Freed from the competitive pressure of a commercial mainstream that might have absorbed and diluted the form's technical escalation. The death metal scene of the early and mid-1990's developed a musical sophistication that represented the most technically advanced heavy music yet produced. Cynic pushing the harmonic language toward jazz-influenced territories no previous form of heavy music had explored. Atheist developing rhythmic complexity that drew on progressive rock's structural sophistication. Gorguts in Canada developed a dissonance and compositional abstraction that pushed the form toward territory contemporary classical music occupying from the opposite direction.

None of this was commercially significant in the conventional sense. The audience was small, specialized, and geographically distributed through the same postal networks the tape trading infrastructure had built in the previous decade. Records sold in quantities the major label infrastructure would have considered commercial failure by the standards it had established. And none of that mattered, because the death metal scene's infrastructure was not designed for major label economics. It was designed for the perpetuation of the form's evolutionary vitality. The escalation for its own sake, the development of musical complexity because musical complexity was what the scene valued and what its infrastructure rewarded.

The fortress and the laboratory had solved the same problem through opposite methods and arrived at the same conclusion. After the Black Album's consolidation, the commercial center of heavy music was no longer the site where the form's most significant evolutionary development was occurring. The significant development was happening at the margins, in the forms that had decided the throne was either contaminating or irrelevant and had built their own spaces accordingly. The fortress insulated through ideology. The laboratory insulated through complexity. Both insulations worked. Both produced music of genuine significance. And both confirmed the structural truth that the Black Album's consolidation had established without intending to — that the commercial center and the evolutionary frontier of heavy music were no longer the same place, and that the distance between them was permanent rather than transitional.

The throne had defined the center. The center had defined

the margins. And the margins had decided the center was someone else's problem.

THE LAST RECOMBINATION (1996-2000)

The center was empty and the emptiness was visible.

By the mid-1990's the commercial landscape of heavy music had the specific quality of a space where something large had recently been removed. The infrastructure was intact, the audience was present, the distribution pipelines were operational, but the artifact that had unified all of it had dissolved into its own success and left behind a field of competing partial solutions. Pantera had the weight and the hostility but not the radio accessibility. The extreme underground had evolutionary vitality but not the commercial scale. Grunge had briefly occupied the mainstream slot but had exhausted itself through the same oversaturation mechanism that had exhausted hair metal. The production aesthetic without the emotional register that had made the original compelling.

MTV was still operational and still powerful but operating with diminished authority. The culture gatekeeping function that had made it the primary driver of commercial music discovery in the mid-1980's. It had been fragmenting since the early 1990's as the channel's programming diversified and the cable infrastructure expanded to offer competing options. Radio had splintered into format niches that served specific demographic segments rather than the broad youth audience FM rock radio had addressed in the previous decade. The arena circuit was still running but increasingly dominated by legacy acts — Metallica, Aerosmith, the surviving hair metal bands with sufficient audience inertia to sustain touring revenue without continued broadcast support.

Into that landscape nu-metal arrived with the specific energy of a form that had identified the empty center and decided to fill it.

Korn's self-titled debut in 1994 established the template, though its commercial impact was gradual rather than immediate. The record building an audience through touring and word-of-mouth before the commercial infrastructure understood what it was dealing with. Life Is Peachy in 1996 expanded the reach. Follow the Leader in 1998 achieved the commercial breakthrough that demonstrated the template's mass viability. It debuted at number one on the Billboard 200, selling over four million copies in the United States, generating the kind of commercial evidence that major labels require before committing the investment.

The structural properties Korn had assembled were a genuine recombination. Not the synthesis thrash had achieved by fusing hardcore and metal's musical properties. A fusion of cultural and rhythmic vocabularies that had not previously occupied the same musical space. The groove metal inheritance was audible in the down-tuned guitar work and the rhythmic authority the low-end emphasis created. The same deceleration from thrash's speed escalation that Pantera had developed but stripped of Pantera's specific abrasiveness and reoriented toward a groove that owed as much to hip-hop's rhythmic vocabulary as to metals. The hip-hop influence was not superficial. It was structural. The rhythmic phrasing of Jonathan Davis's vocal delivery drawing on the cadence patterns rap had developed. Drum programming and rhythmic feel of the instrumental tracks carrying a bounce and a syncopation that metal's four-on-the-floor tradition had never incorporated. The emotional register was the crucial differentiator. Not the controlled authority of the Black Album, not the hostile aggression of Pantera, not the atmospheric extremity of black metal. A vulnerability and a psychological directness about damage and dysfunction that no previous form of heavy music had been willing to occupy at commercial scale.

That emotional register was the key to nu-metal's specific commercial achievement and the source of its specific subcultural failure. The vulnerability worked commercially because it addressed an emotional experience. Adolescent alienation, family dysfunction, psychological damage, the specific pain of being young and not knowing what to do with the feelings that entailed. Korn, Limp Bizkit, Slipknot, and Deftones were making music that their audience recognized as being about them. In a way that the Black Album's authoritative command and Pantera's hostile aggression and the extreme underground's various forms of ideological extremity had not been. The recognition generated the most durable form of audience loyalty that popular music can generate. The loyalty of an audience that has found the music that finally sounds like its own internal experience.

The subcultural failure was the mirror image of commercial success. The metal community's rejection of nu-metal was not simply aesthetic conservatism. It was a structural response to a form that had achieved commercial scale by abandoning the specific properties the metal tradition had established as the markers of seriousness. The absence of guitar solos was the most frequently cited grievance and the least important one analytically. The guitar solo's suppression was a consequence of the hip-hop influence's rhythmic reorientation rather than a deliberate rejection of technical capacity. The more significant structural grievance was the simplification of the harmonic and rhythmic vocabulary. The reduction of the riff's compositional function to a groove delivery mechanism rather than a structural and harmonic statement. The prioritization of rhythmic feel over musical content in a way that the metal tradition's riff-centered compositional logic could not accommodate without ceasing to be itself.

Limp Bizkit made the subcultural failure more visible than any other nu-metal act because of Fred Durst's specific persona. The backward cap, the aggressive commercial ambition, the deliberate courting of the mainstream's attention without any apparent awareness that the mainstream's attention was supposed to be complicated. He embodied the form's relationship to the commercial infrastructure in a way the metal community found impossible to accept. Durst was not performing discomfort with commercial success the way Cobain had. He was not maintaining the studied indifference to the commercial machinery that Hetfield had developed into a form of authority. He was enthusiastically, visibly, unashamedly pursuing commercial success as a primary goal, and the pursuit was successful enough. Significant Other in 1999 selling over sixteen million copies worldwide. The metal community's rejection registered as irrelevant to the commercial infrastructure's assessment of what nu-metal was achieving.

The Deftones occupied the most interesting position within the nu-metal commercial moment because they were the form's internal critique. A band working within the same general musical territory as Korn and Limp Bizkit but pushing its textural and atmospheric properties in directions that pointed toward the post-nu-metal landscape rather than toward the commercial center the form was attempting to occupy. Around the Fur in 1997 and White Pony in 2000 demonstrated that the nu-metal recombination's basic elements. The down-tuned rhythmic weight, the hip-hop rhythmic influence, the emotional vulnerability could be developed toward genuine musical sophistication rather than commercial optimization. The Deftones were not commercially marginal. White Pony sold significantly and generated genuine critical attention. They were commercially adjacent to nu-metal rather than central to it. The band's specific musical intelligence pulling them out of the commercial center's gravity toward more complex and less immediately legible territory.

Slipknot arrived in 1999 and demonstrated that the nu-metal commercial moment had room for a form of the recombination that pushed the extreme metal variables significantly further than Korn or Limp Bizkit had been willing to go. The nine-member lineup, the masks, the percussive density of the two-drummer and two-percussionist rhythm section. The guitar work carrying death metal's tonal aggression into a commercial framework that the death metal scene had specifically constructed to resist commercial absorption. The masks were the nu-metal era's most significant visual innovation. Not the self-explanatory spectacle of hair metal's image and not the deliberate repulsion of black metal's corpse paint but something between them. A visual identity that was immediately striking and simultaneously resistant to the kind of demographic legibility that MTV's visual economy had historically required. The masks communicated intensity and anonymity. Here we are, you cannot know us. The combination proved commercially viable in a way that the extreme underground's visual philosophy had always insisted it couldn't be.

What nu-metal's commercial moment confirmed, across all its variants and all its commercial achievements and all its subcultural failures, was the structural truth that the Black Album's dissolution had established. Recombination could restore commercial gravity. The center could be partially refilled by a form of sufficient ambition and sufficient alignment with the current moment's emotional requirements. But the specific convergence of every distribution pipeline around a single artifact with unified legitimacy across every segment of the heavy music audience. The convergence that had defined the throne could not be rebuilt by recombination alone. Because the infrastructure that had made the convergence possible had fragmented and the fragmentation was not a temporary condition awaiting the right artifact to resolve it.

Nu-metal unified MTV and arenas. It did not unify MTV, arenas, FM radio, the metal subcultural audience, the extreme underground's various communities, and the hardcore infrastructure. It captured some of those pipelines and was rejected by others, and the rejection was not a failure of execution. Not a case of the wrong recombination or the wrong production or the wrong emotional register. A structural consequence of the permanently diversified landscape that heavy music had become. The extreme underground communities had built their own infrastructure and their own audience and their own definition of what the music was. That infrastructure was now sufficiently robust it did not need the commercial mainstream's validation and did not respond to its gravitational pull. The hardcore community had its own circuit and its own economics and its own values that the commercial mainstream had never successfully absorbed. The metal traditionalist community had its own standards and its own canon and its own understanding of what technical and compositional seriousness required that nu-metal's simplifications had specifically violated.

The throne required unanimous recognition. Nu-metal achieved majority recognition among the youth audience that MTV and the arena circuit addressed. Minority recognition or active rejection from every other district. That was not a throne. It was a commercial phenomenon — significant, genuine, in some cases musically interesting, in all cases historically important. Not a structural centralization of heavy music around a unified identity. The Black Album had been the last of those. Nu-metal was the proof that the last had been the last.

By 2000 nu-metal was already showing the structural fatigue that hair metal had shown in 1990. The form's conventions becoming codified, the visual and sonic markers becoming legible as genre requirements rather than genuine expressions. The audience beginning the slow withdrawal that precedes every commercial form collapse into artifact. The withdrawal this time was different in kind from every previous withdrawal. The infrastructure the audience was withdrawing into was not a new commercial center waiting to be discovered but a permanently fragmented landscape of specialized communities. Each with its own music and its own infrastructure and its own definition of what heaviness meant.

MULTIPOLAR PERMANENCE (1998-2000)

By 2000 the argument this book has been building since Birmingham had reached its conclusion. Not a dramatic conclusion — no decisive battle, no definitive victory, no single moment when the outcome became clear. The conclusion was quieter and more permanent than any of those. It was the moment when a form that had spent thirty years cycling through centralization and fragmentation and re-centralization simply stopped cycling. The fragmentation became permanent condition. The mutation became the product. The center stopped being the goal.

This is easy to misread as decline. It is not decline. Heavy music in 2000 was not smaller than it had been in 1991. It was no less vital, less innovative, less capable of producing music of genuine significance and genuine emotional power. It was larger than it had ever been. More globally distributed, more technically sophisticated across more forms, more deeply embedded in more distinct communities with more robust independent infrastructures than any previous phase. What had ended was not heavy music's vitality. What had ended was the specific historical condition under which a single form of heavy music could define what all heavy music was.

Map the landscape as it existed in the century's close.

Black metal had completed its transformation from a localized Norwegian ideological project into a global form with regional variants. Swedish, American, French, each carrying the fortress's basic architecture into new geographic and cultural contexts. Developing specific properties that reflected the local conditions in which the music was being made. The fortress had replicated itself across continents without losing its essential insulation from the commercial mainstream. No major label. No MTV rotation. No FM radio. Just the postal networks and the independent label infrastructure the underground had been building since the hardcore era, now supplemented by early internet file-sharing and the web forums beginning to replace the zine networks as the primary medium of scene communication and critical discourse.

Death metal had completed its specialization into multiple

parallel technical trajectories. The Florida scene's brutality-focused development running alongside the Swedish melodic death metal scene's harmonic sophistication. Running alongside the progressive experiments of Cynic and Atheist and Gorguts. Each trajectory pursuing its own escalation logic with competitive awareness and independence from commercial pressure. The laboratory was running multiple experiments and they were not converging. They were diverging — each pursuing the specific variables that its practitioners found most musically interesting. The divergence producing a richness and variety of musical development that the commercial mainstream's homogenizing logic had never been capable of generating.

Pantera had proven that hostile authority could sustain arena-scale commercial success through a decade of consistent output without radio accessibility or visual economic compliance. The touring infrastructure they had built — the specific relationship between a band of genuine heaviness and an audience of genuine scale. All sustained through the live circuit rather than through broadcast media. A template for commercial sustainability that the post-throne landscape had made newly viable. You did not need MTV's rotation to fill arenas if you had built the audience through touring over a sufficient period. You needed the music to be heavy enough and consistent enough and honest enough that the audience kept coming back. Pantera had demonstrated this. The demonstration was as consequential for the post-2000 landscape as the Black Album's demonstration of controlled authority had been for the post-1991 landscape.

Nu-metal was completing its commercial arc with the specific efficiency the major label infrastructure applied to every commercial form it had identified. It reproduced at scale, and exhausted through oversaturation. The visual and sonic markers had become genre requirements. The major label investment that had followed Follow the Leader and Significant Other's commercial breakthroughs had produced a second and third wave of nu-metal acts carrying the template's surface properties without the specific emotional authenticity that had made the template compelling. The backward cap and the down-tuned guitar and the hip-hop vocal cadence as costume rather than expression. The vulnerability as performance rather than genuine exposure. The audience was noticing. By 2001 and 2002 the withdrawal would accelerate into the form's commercial collapse. All while following the same structural logic that every previous commercial collapse in heavy music's history had followed. Oversaturation producing fatigue, fatigue producing the search for contrast, the search for contrast finding what the commercial mainstream had been ignoring while it reproduced the successful template.

What the commercial mainstream had been ignoring was metalcore. The synthesis that the hardcore and metal communities had been developing through the second half of the 1990s in the same underground spaces and through the same independent infrastructure that every previous significant mutation had emerged from before commercial attention arrived. Converge's Jane Doe in 2001. Killswitch Engage's Alive or Just Breathing in 2002. The forms were assembling their commercial moment while nu-metal was exhausting its own. The timing replicating the pattern that had run from arena rock to punk to hardcore to thrash to hair metal to grunge to the Black Album to nu-metal. The next mutation always developing in the underground while the current commercial center occupied the mainstream's attention. Always arriving at commercial visibility at the moment when the current center's exhaustion created the opening.

But metalcore's commercial moment, when it arrived, would be shorter than nu-metal's, which had been shorter than grunge's, which had been shorter than hair metal's. The acceleration of the cycle was a consequence of the infrastructure's permanent diversification. The major label reproduction mechanism has not changed. The audience's capacity for oversaturation had not changed. What had changed was the speed of information transfer and the depth of the alternative infrastructure. The internet was dissolving the geographic isolation that had always given underground scenes the developmental time they needed to mature before commercial attention arrived. Which meant the commercial infrastructure was finding new forms faster, reproducing them faster, and exhausting them faster. The cycle was accelerating toward the point where it would become too fast to produce stable commercial forms at all.

That acceleration is the story of heavy music after 2000. But it begins here — in the permanent fragmentation of the landscape as it existed in the century's close. In the specific conditions that the thirty-year arc from Birmingham to the

Black Album to multipolar permanence had produced and left behind as its legacy.

The legacy was this. Heavy music had demonstrated, across thirty years of escalation and mutation and commercial exploitation and underground resistance and re-centralization and fragmentation, that it was not a genre with fixed properties and a stable identity but a force. A set of structural energies that different communities in various places under different pressures had channeled into different forms. Each form legitimate on its own terms, each carrying the fundamental properties of amplification and weight and physical impact that Birmingham had first formalized while deploying those properties in the service of whatever the specific community's specific historical moment required. Dread when the historical moment required dread. Confrontation when it required confrontation. Celebration when it requires celebration. Technical escalation when the internal logic demanded escalation. Atmospheric withdrawal when the external pressure demanded withdrawal. Hostile authority, when controlled authority had become too comfortable to sustain the music's essential tension with the world.

No single form had been the true form. No single community had owned the definition. The underground's insistence on purity had been as much a historical artifact as hair metal's spectacle. both responses to specific pressures, both valid on their own terms, both temporary. What persisted was not any specific form but the underlying force.

— The specific human need for music heavy enough to be felt

rather than merely heard, that engaged the body before the mind, which created communities around the shared experience of physical and emotional intensity. The commercial mainstream's optimized accessibility had always been designed to minimize.

That need had not diminished by 2000. It had multiplied. The communities that had formed around heavy music's various forms were larger and more globally distributed and more deeply embedded in more distinct cultural contexts than at any previous point in the form's history. The infrastructure those communities had built — the independent labels and touring circuits and zine networks transitioning to web forums and the file-sharing networks beginning to dissolve the last remnants of geographic isolation. More robust and more self-sustaining than it had ever been.

Heavy music had not become mass in the sense of achieving permanent unified dominance. It had become mass in the sense of becoming too large and too various and too deeply rooted in too many communities to be contained by any single definition or controlled by any single infrastructure or exhausted by any single commercial cycle. The throne was gone. The competing kingdoms remained — each sovereign, each vital, each carrying the fundamental force forward into the next century in the specific form that its specific community had developed to carry it.

Birmingham had formalized the dread. The dread had become a force. The force had become a movement. The movement had become a world.

The world did not need a king.

It needed what it had always needed. The next mutation, the next escalation, the next room where someone was making something heavier than anything that had existed before. Not because the infrastructure demanded it or the commercial logic required it. The critical consensus had identified it as the necessary next step. Because the music demanded it and the community that had gathered around the music had built the infrastructure to carry it. The human need that had generated the music in the first place had not diminished and would not diminish and could not diminish because it was not a taste or a preference or a cultural moment.

It was a permanent condition of being human in a world that required, periodically and urgently and without apology, something that hit hard enough to be real.

And this is where the argument ends, and where the story continues. That thirty-year arc from Birmingham to multipolar permanence has been mapped by the structural forces that have transformed heaviness from a local mutation into a global condition — the economics, infrastructure, escalation logic, the centralization cycles, the underground's perpetual resistance to definition, the commercial mainstream's perpetual attempt to impose it. Because the story after 2000 takes on a distinctive character requiring a different book. The internet dissolving the last geographic barriers, the algorithm replacing the A&R executive as the primary discovery mechanism, the streaming economy restructuring the financial logic of every infrastructure that this text has been covering, the global proliferation of micro-scenes making the tape trading network look primitive by comparison. The force persists. The mutation continues. The next envelope is already in the mail.

270